SOPHISTRY AND
TWENTIETH-CENTURY ART

Haim Gordon
and
Rivca Gordon

Rodopi

Amsterdam – New York, NY 2002

The paper on which this book is printed meets the requirements of "ISO
9706:1994, Information and documentation - Paper for documents -
Requirements for permanence".

ISBN: 90-420-1529-2
©Editions Rodopi B.V., Amsterdam – New York, NY 2002
Printed in The Netherlands

SOPHISTRY AND
TWENTIETH-CENTURY ART

VIBS

Volume 123

Robert Ginsberg
Executive Editor

Associate Editors

This book is dedicated to:

The memory of our dear friend Dieter Ameln who would have stood and laughed at many of the manifestation of sophistry in twentieth-century art that we criticize.

Our dear friend Marianne Ameln whose love for truth, joy in life, and generosity stand in direct contradiction to the works of sophistry in twentieth-century art.

CONTENTS

FOREWORD

Twentieth-century and contemporary art introduced beside beauty, truth and authenticity, falseness, destruction and ugliness, as legitimate components of art. Relating to what is beautiful and true in art becomes harder and harder, as fakery and deceit characterizes so much of this century's art works.

Sophistry and Twentieth-Century Art, by Haim Gordon and Rivca Gordon, presents us with a new-old way of relating truthfully toward what is true in art.

Falseness in art was pointed out centuries ago by Plato's philosophy. The Platonic name for fakeries in art was called sophistry. Since then, till the twentieth century, relating to the truth in art was often synonymous to seeking out what was beautiful in these creations. Looking for beauty in art meant also relating authentically toward the truth and authenticity in the work of art. Twentieth-century and contemporary art, besides its few brilliant creations, presented the world with fake, shallow, seductive, pseudo consumer's products, which are falsely called art. These sophistries are ruinous to human existence.

Haim Gordon and Rivca Gordon underline the beauty in a work of art, and how is it connected with what is truthful in art. By concentrating on the insights and ideas of two of the most prominent philosophers of the twentieth century, Martin Heidigger and Nicolas Berdyaev, the Gordons point out once again the importance of the revealing of truth and beauty in art. They teach us how this way of relating toward art can enhance and better human existence.

Unfortunately, art critics today enlarge the rift between art and human being, by supporting falseness and deceit in art. Furthermore, they usually support the fact that art has no necessary connections with beauty, truth, or what Plato called the good. Thus, they give a "learned" justification for this severance to occur.

Why do human beings long for beauty and truth? And why can great works of art contribute toward creativity, responsibility, and independence in our mode of existence? How are works of art involved with personality and personal freedom?

By discussing very carefully Heidigger's major essay, "The Origin of the Work of Art," and Berdyaev's book, *Slavery and Freedom,* the Gordons are responding with originality to these major questions. *Sophistry and Twentieth-Century Art* reveals the challenging possibilities of discovering again what is beauty and truth in art, and how art can be a source for the good in human existence.

Rina Shtelman
Kay Teachers College

INTRODUCTION

> For when evils are far gone and irremediable, the task
> of censuring them is never pleasant, although at times
> necessar.
>
> Plato, *The Laws*, 660

In *Art*, a highly successful short one-act play written by Yasmina Reza, one of the characters, Serge, purchases a Minimalist painting in which the canvas is all painted white and, if you look carfully, on the white background, you can see white diagonal lines. When Serge shows this painting, for which he paid two hundred thousand francs, to Marc, his closest friend, Marc is flabbergasted. Marc's response is that the painting is "shit"[1] The play shows how the relationship between Marc and Serge deteriorates through their different responses to the white painting, and also to each other as persons relating to the painting.

We believe that in her brilliant comedy, Reza has put her finger on one of the prominent fakeries of the twentieth century. We call this fakery that has emerged in the visual arts by its Platonic name, sophistry. Learning from Plato and from other great thinkers, in the chapters of this book we unmask and condemn the sophistry that has come to characterize much of twentieth-century visual art; we also briefly confront, unmask, and condemn some of the writings on twentieth-century art that accompany and applaud these works of fake art.

This book is not merely an attack on sophistry in the contemporary visual arts. Our rejection of sophistry is presented together with brief descriptions of what can be learned on how to relate to art from the thinking and the ideas of two great twentieth-century philosophers, Martin Heidegger and Nicolas Berdyaev. Both thinkers have enlightened us as to what constitutes a beautiful work of art, and how an authentic relation to the beauty in a work of art enhances human existence.

At the outset, we want to be clear that our rejection of sophistry in twentieth-century visual art should not suggest that we condemn all works of visual art produced in the twentieth century. On the contrary, we firmly believe that many great twentieth-century artists created glorious and beautiful works of art. Among these great artists are Pablo Picasso, Georges Braque, Balthus, Lucien Freud, Francis Bacon, Frank Lloyd Wright, Henri Matisse, Marc Chagall, Pierre Bonnard, Alice Neel, Georges Rouault, Otto Dix, Egon Schiele, Edward Hopper, Diego Rivera. But for the frequent museum visitor, the beautiful works of these and many other worthy artists often seem sidelined by the ongoing multifarious displays of works of sophistry. Prominent among the creators of the works of fake art which crowd museums and galleries are Marcel Duchamp, Piet Mondrian, many of the surrealists, many of the futurists, Joan Miro, Jasper Johns, Andy Warhol, Mark Rothko, Roy Lichtenstein, Jackson Pollock, the Minimalists, the Pop Artists, the Installationists, the Conceptualists — to mention several of the producers of fake art and some of the approaches that encouraged the production of works of fake art.

Unfortunately, as Reza intimates in her comedy, these works of sophistry that masquerade as art are supported by hosts of art critics, pseudo-thinkers, and other major and minor sophists. As we will soon show by our citing of a few sentences from two such sophists, these critics and psuedo-thinkers fit Plato's definition of the sophist as a person who has the ability to insidiously present Being as non-Being and non-Being as Being. Plato shows that by engaging in such insidiousness and deceit, the sophist strives to seduce people to believe in unproved opinions and to eradicate the quest for truth .d knowledge.

For instance, in his dialogue, *Greater Hippias*, Plato describes the sophist, Hippias, attempting to convince Socrates to accept his foolish views about beauty. With more than a bit of irony, Socrates questions these views. Their dialogue reveals that the highly successful Hippias knows nothing about the essence of beauty. In the twentieth century, Heidegger often attacked sophistry. In one instance, he noted that the sophist

> does not strive for genuine understanding, has no perseverence, but only nibbles on everything, always on the newest and usually on what is in fact worthwhile, but he only nibbles on it and is seduced into mere curiosity and bluffing. He is not one who seeks to understand, i.e., not the one who truly understands. He is rather the rationalizer for whom nothing is certain....[2]

The following chapters will suggest that many contemporary art critics and art historians continue in the tradition of sophistry exemplified by Plato's Hippias. They know nothing about the essence of beauty, nor about the essence of the work of art, yet they succeed in conveying their foolish rhetoric about works of art to all and sundry. As Heidegger noted, these sophists do not strive for geuine understanding. Nor do they strive for truth. They nibble on everything new, and usually on what is worthwhile, and play with their seductions and bluffing.

Thus, we shall hold that those vain, yet seductive art critics, who laud and applaud works of sophistry in twentieth-century art, are not only enemies of truth, knowledge, beauty, and wisdom. Like Plato's Hippias, these twentieth-century sophists also contribute to the alienation and to the erosion of spi-rituality, an erosion that has emerged in much of twentieth-century visual art.

We believe that you can trace many of the expressions of sophistry in twentieth-century visual art to one basic idea. In simple language, this idea states: a work of art has no necessary relationship to beauty. It does not have to be beautiful.

From this idea come many additional questionable ideas, that seemingly justify accepting works of sophistry as art. Here are a few of the more popular among these questionable ideas: art is merely a subjective manner of expressing feelings; art is sheer creativity; non-art is art; art is there to merely arouse the viewer's moods, tastes, and feelings; art is a matter of taste and opinion; art is empty — you put into it what you wish; art is an expression of the popular and democratic trends in contemporary society, hence, say, Andy Warhol's painting of a can of Campbell's Soup best expresses these trends; the role of art is to unmask the deceit of our society; art is for art's sake; art should arouse simple aesthetic enjoyment; art should thrill.

What unites all of these slogans, and many other pseudo-ideas promoted by prominent art historians, by so-called philosophers of art, by some historians of art, by popular art critics, and by journalists who cover art exhibitions? Furthermore, what unites these slogans and pseudo-ideas with the thousands of works of sophistry produced by many pseudo-artists that are exhibited in museums and galleries? They are united by the underlying belief that neither the viewer, nor the critic should approach the work of art with the expectation of encountering something beautiful .

We firmly reject all the above slogans and psuedo-ideas, albeit in this book we will not relate to them individually. Learning from great thinkers of the past such as Plato, Hegel, and Heidegger, we hold that the divorce of beauty from art is wrong, because beauty is essential to art. We have also learned from many great thinkers of the past that the divorce of beauty from art is an eradication of a major dimension of human spirituality. These seminal thinkers indicated clearly that beauty, together with wisdom, justice, love, knowledge, and other things that are worthy in themselves, are central to human spirituality. Consequently, creativity, feelings, taste, or aesthetic enjoyment may, at times, accompany spirituality, but they are not central to it.

For instance, people can engage their creativity to construct effective means of destroying their fellow human beings. Creating an efficient gas chamber to kill human beings is not an act of spirituality. For creativity to be linked to spirituality it must relate to things that are worthy in themselves, such as justice, beauty, knowledge, love, or wisdom. What is more, quite a few great thinkers have stated what many a person experiences when he or she encounters a lovely painting by Vermeer or a glorious sculpture by Michelangelo — that the beauty of a work of art can be a great source of inspiration for a person's daily and spiritual existence.

Hence, the divorcing of art from beauty, as has happened in many contemporary works of art that are displayed in museums is, at best, an act of sophistry. More likely, it is a cynical attempt to destroy what Plato called the Good, which, he believed, illuminates our spiritual existence in the manner that the sun illuminates our physical life. Such a destructive tendency in many realms of twentieth-century art fits well with many destructive trends of our life that are daily promoted by the princes of twentieth-century corporate capitalism. In the later chapters of this book, we briefly assess and reject the spiritual wasteland and the bizarre sophistry spread by these princes of corporate capitalism and by their many intellectual sycophants. We especially relate to the role of these princes in spreading sophistry in much of twentieth-century art. We also describe some of the links between the spread and the acceptance of works of sophistry in twentieth-century art, by many curators at museums and by lay people, and the spiritual wasteland promoted by the princes of the corporate capitalist regime.

In educating and encouraging his contemporaries to relate to the Good, which included the beauty that the muses inspired, Plato was always aware of the dangers of sophistry. Hence in preparation for writing this book we undertook a careful reading of Plato's dialogues. We found in them truths that will help us to unmask and to reject the sophistry that emerges in twentieth century visual arts, and in the writings of many of its prominent promoters. In *Sophist*, for instance, Plato defines the sophist and describes the dangers of his art of seduction. Indeed, in all of Plato's dialogues that deal with sophistry, and especially in *Gorgias* and *Sophist*, the sophist is not a true philosopher or educator; he is a seducer (in ancient Greece, all sophists were males). We have learned much from Plato, yet this book is not a presentation of all of his ideas on sophistry or on art. For instance, we do not relate Plato's discussion of art in *The Republic*.

Note that the word "seduction," which Plato describes as central to all sophistry, can pretty well describe Serge's relation to the white canvas that he has purchased in the play, *Art*. Serge has *not* been attracted to the beauty of the white canvas that he purchased; he never suggests that it is beautiful. Nor has Serge discovered an important truth that has become unconcealed in the totally white painting. Instead, Serge has been seduced to believe that this totally white canvas is a very important piece of art, well worth the two hundred thousand francs that he spent to obtain it. He explains to Marc that he can already resell it at a profit. We therefore repeat: Learning from Plato, and from our encounters with these works, we suggest that many contemporary works of sophistry in art are essentially seductive .

In another attack in *Sophist*, Plato describes the sophist as a dissembler of truth, a juggler of words, and an imitator of appearances. Subsequent chapters will show that the twentieth-century producers of fake art are indeed sophists, in Plato's sense of the word. At present, two questions arise which help us to address twentieth century art. Is great art linked to truth? If so, how is beauty linked to truth ?

Plato answered the first question with a resounding: Yes! Great art must be linked to truth. The first question was also answered in the affirmative, explicitly and implicitly, by quite a few twentieth-century thinkers, among them Heidegger, Buber, and Berdyaev. These contemporary thinkers differ in their answers to the second question. As mentioned, in this book we bring some of the responses to these questions by Heidegger and by Berdyaev.

But, you need not necessarily adhere to what a thinker says to answer the first question posed above. You can simply comprehend a great work of art, say, Edward Hopper's beautiful and haunting painting called "Nighthawks." For truths to emerge, all you need to do is to look and to be sensitive to what you see in "Nighthawks." You will soon perceive the sadness of human alienation, aloneness, and loneliness. If you look longer additional truths about human existence and a person's quest for companionship and meaning will slowly emerge. Furthermore, while looking carefully at this painting, and comprehending some of the insights of the above three thinkers, you may find that all three thinkers may contribute substantially to answering the question concerning the links between beauty and truth.

A glance at some of the many ways of expressing sophistry that appear in twentieth century works of art shows how they cause the two major questions formulated in the preceding paragraph to vanish. There is no meaning to the question: Is great art linked to truth? when you consider a Minimalist painting, such as the white canvas purchased by Serge, or one of Piet Mondrian's paintings of colored lines and squares. Nor is there a meaning to this question when you look at one of Andy Warhol's canvases of cans of Campbell's Soup, or at Jasper Johns's paintings of the American flag or of targets. We are saying that if you look carefully at a painting by Rembrandt or by Van Gogh or by Hopper, truths about human existence are disclosed to you. However, even if for hours you gaze at a Minimalist painting, or at a Warhol canvas of a can of Campbell's Soup, or at the flags and targets painted by Jasper Johns, no truths emerge. Nothing.

Widespread sophistry, in relation to truth, is also found in the writings of many prominent art critics, journalists who cover art exhibitions, thinkers on contemporary art, historians of contemporary art, and many others. Can one be a writer who supports works of fake art without oneself becoming a sophist? We doubt it!

Such sophistry is hardly a new phenomenon in twentieth-century art criticism, and journalism, as you will discover if you peruse, say, Harold Rosenberg's shallow and foolish book *The Tradition of the New*, first published in 1959.[3] Rosenberg was an art critic for *The New Yorker*, and his book is a collection of his essays, some of which were written in the 1930s. *The Tradition of the New* went through many printings, hence Rosenberg's superficial approach to life and to art, and his multiple inanities, may have served as an example for many contemporary art critics, journalists, and historians, whose writings are works of sophistry. Here is a brief, recent example of such sophistry, written lately, but in the tradition of foolishness found in Rosenberg's wriitngs.

One acclaimed and famous writer on contemporary art is Arthur C. Danto, winner of the 1990 National Book Critic Circle Award for criticism. Danto is currently the art critic of the liberal weekly, *The Nation*. He has written a few books on contemporary art. Danto was also, until he retired, an acclaimed and lauded professor of philosophy at Columbia University. Consider a few sentences from Danto's book *The Visual Arts in Post-Historical Perspective* .

> There is, of course, a difference between art and non-art, between works of art and what I like to refer to as "mere real things." What Warhol taught was that there is no way of telling the difference by mere looking. The eye, so prized an aesthetic organ when it was felt that the difference between art and non-art was visible, was philosophically of no use whatever when the difference proved invisible.[4]

So the difference between art and non-art in the visual arts has been "proved invisible" In this vein, Danto could add that the difference between Mozart's 40th symphony and the screeching of a cat in heat has been proved inaudible .

There is no need to comment at any length on such stupidity, except by calling it sophistry of the cheapest brand. We blush at the need to repeat simple truths such as the following. Visual arts are something that we relate to primordially with our eyes, our bodily vision; music is something that we relate to primordially with our ears, our bodily hearing. Blind people cannot relate to visual arts. For them, the distinction between art and non-art is invisible. Deaf people can only rarely, with their body, relate to music. Therefore, if the difference between art and non-art has "proved invisible," nothing is left for the visitor at a museum or for the art critic, such as Danto, to look at, to relate to, and to discuss .

After considering the above cited ideas, we wonder if the astute philosopher, Danto, would also state that the difference between love and non-love has been "proved invisible?" And what about the difference between justice and non-justice? Probably that has been proved incomprehensible.

Consequently, Danto's above statements of cheap sophistry are also smug. His statement that the difference between art and non-art has been proved invisible is merely a renewed instance of the sophist's attempts, which Plato harshly condemned, to attribute Being to non-Being and non Being to Being. Danto, who was a respected professor of philosophy undoubtedly read Plato's *Sophist;* but, he learned nothing from this great dialogue. Yet even without reading Plato, Danto should know that any so called work of art whose distinction from non-art is invisible is a fake .

Another example of smugness by a supposedly famous thinker on art can be found in Jacques Barzun's book *The Use and Abuse of Art*.[5] The book is based on what Barzun taught when, in 1973, he was chosen to give the highly regarded series of A.W. Mellon Lectures on the topic of art at the National Gallery of Art in Washington, D.C. In his lectures, Barzun attempts to support many of the works of sophistry that have appeared in twentieth century art.

We do not want to discuss Barzun's many brazen statements that are mere sophistry, since they appear quite frequently in his book, much as they appear in many other books by writers on contemporary art. But Barzun's smugness, his superciliousness, and his chutzpah are quite unique; they are a bane to the search for truth and to genuine intellectual life. One sentence from the entire book suffices to reveal this smugness, superciliousness, and chutzpah; we could bring at least a dozen. Barzun writes: "I shall suggest later on why Western Civilization has not had a new idea in fifty years."[6]

Let us be precise. Jacques Barzun's above sentence was stated in 1973. In it he held that "Western Civilization has not had a new idea in fifty years." Fortunately, history shows otherwise. Forty-six years earlier, in 1927, Heidegger published *Being and Time* in Germany. Put succinctly, *Being* and *Time* is broadly acknowledged as a text abounding in new ideas and thoughts. In the late 1930s and early 1940s, Jean-Paul Sartre appeared on the philosophical and literary scene of France and the world, bringing with him dozens of new ideas that, like Heidegger's groundbreaking ideas, have become central to Western civilization. And did Barzun never hear of the new, original, and revolutionary ideas of the Austrian/British thinker, Ludwig Wittgenstein, published in the 1940s and 1950s? We could go on and include the thinking of Albert Einstein, Niels Bohr, or Werner Heisenberg; we could mention some of their breathtaking new ideas that were published after 1923 — but we can stop here. Barzun's above statement, like many other statements in his book, is false.

The falseness of Barzun's statement is of less concern, however, than the superciliousness, the smugness, and the downright chutzpah of the author to which the sentence testifies. Barzun writes as if he were God. Like the divine Being, or the God of history, Barzun knows "why Western Civilization has not had a new idea in fifty years." But it is but one step from the sublime to the ridiculous, and Barzun has gone much more than one step in this direction. For instance, his thoughts on art and religion, and on other topics are unsubstanitated, inane, and, yes, often stupid and ridiculous. They are so far from the truth that they are not even worth refuting.

By the way, writers on twentieth-century art who support works of fake art and who write similarly to Barzun are common. Indeed, you will find many such supercilious writers, who spread falsehoods, among the staunch

supporters of the works of sophistry in twentieth-century art. A few examples
of such writing will be found in the chapters of this book.

We do not believe that rejecting the sophistry in twentieth-century art
requires writing a voluminous text. The issues are quite simple. As Socrates
repeatedly explained, truth can often be seen clearly when a person decides to
seek it. Put differently, this is a short book because, since beauty shines out
and is admired for itself, since beauty does not need to be explained or
justified, attacking ugliness, shallowness, and indifference does not require
many profound or broad explanations. Once the marvelous role of beauty and
truth in the work of art, and in human existence, is evident, ugly and shallow
works of fake art merely need to be pointed to, scorned, and firmly rejected.
We will only partially describe the ruinous effects of the works of fake art for
individuals and for society at large.

Because we decided to write a short book that will present our
rejection of sophistry in twentieth-century art, we decided not to present a
historical survey of what great thinkers, say Kant and Hegel wrote about art.
Instead, we chose to concentrate on a few of the insights and ideas proffered
by only two major twentieth-century thinkers, Heidegger and Berdyaev. We
could have chosen quite a number of other worthy thinkers, such as Martin
Buber, Paul Tillich, and Gabriel Marcel to reject the sophistry that we are
attacking. Yet we found that the thinking of Heidegger and Berdyaev accorded
the closest to our own ideas and to the relations that we have established with
great works of art. Hence their thinking also supports our firm rejection of
sophistry. In what follows, the challenging thoughts and insights that we will
glean from Heidegger and Berdyaev will be supported by our own impressions
when relating to great works of art — say, paintings by Vermeer and Matisse —
and by our personal responses to twentieth-century works of sophistry.

In Chapters One and Three, we discuss a major essay by Heidegger,
"The Origin of the Work of Art." Chapter Two is a brief interlude that points
to the fact that Heidegger's essay is based on the belief that human beings long
for beauty and truth .In "The Origin of the Work of Art," Heidegger carefully
links the genuine work of art to beauty and to the unconcealing of truth. In
both chapters, we learn from Heidegger's insights and thoughts while relating
his thinking to what happened in the realm of art in this past century. This
approach helps us to apprehend the insidious links between the attempt to
banish truth and beauty from art and the sophistry that emerges in twentieth
century art. Thus, the first three chapters of this book help to clarify, albeit
partially, why and how great art is beautiful and how only great works of art
can unconceal certain truths that are significant to human existence. In
addition, while learning from Heidegger and relating to twentieth-century art,
we will again emphasize the point made by Plato and by other great thinkers:
Beauty in art is crucial for truth and for a worthy human existence.

Chapter Four describes and discusses the indifference that emanates
from many of the works of sophistry in twentieth-century art that are found in

museums and galleries, for instance, the indifference that emanates from Piet Mondrian's abstract paintings or from many Minimalist paintings. It also suggests, briefly, how this widespread indifference, that emanates from the many works of fake art in museums, is destructive both for art and for human existence.

The thinking of Berdyaev on the riddle and the mystery of personality, as expressed in his book *Slavery and Freedom*, is presented in Chapter Five. On the basis of Berdyaev's insights, we explain why the works of sophistry in twentieth-century art are ruinous for the human quest for freedom and genuine creativity; we also clarify why these works of sophistry help to undermine the challenge which each person faces to live as a personality, and not as an enslaved individual. We learn from Berdyaev that, in contrast to works of sophistry, great works of art will often constitute a major contribution to a person's personality and to his or her freedom and creativity .

Learning further from Berdyaev, in Chapter Six we indicate that the works of sophistry in twentieth-century art are egocentric and ruinous of personality. Focusing on Minimalist so-called works of art, while relying on the wisdom of Søren Kierkegaard, we also suggest that these works are vacuous and spiritually barren .

Works of fake art, like the painting that Serge purchased, spread and sustain superficiality. They thus ruin all spirituality, primarily by invading culture and lowering it to an inane, and often infantile common denominator. To briefly point to this evident finding is the theme of Chapter Seven. In that chapter, we rely on some of Marcel Proust's enlightening ideas concerning the relations between a worthy work of art and the truths of a person's being. We also point out that works of fake art have attempted to invade all realms of human culture, and have endeavored to convert these realms of culture into realms of mere entertainment. By succeeding in these invasions, many works of sophistry have often succeeded in legitimizing their own shallowness and vacuity. The result is that this spread of superficiality wreaks havoc upon all genuine spirituality.

In Chapter Eight, we turn to Berdyaev's discussion of the dialectic of master and slave, which he contrasts to the life of a free person. We discuss Berdyaev's statement that persons love to be enslaved, and we link the statement to the spread of works of fake art. Learning from Berdyaev, we hold that both the master and the slave refuse to relate to the mystery of beauty, and are constantly enslaved by the objectification, exteriorization, and rationalization of everything spiritual. They are also enslaved by many additional personality-destructive lures of contemporary life. Such enslavement also ruins the ongoing struggle for social justice that some free persons may undertake. Hence, we find a close link between the spread of masters and slaves, which includes the prominence of the master-slave dialectic in the twentieth century, and the prominence given to works of fake art — which are among the lures that destroy personality.

Chapter Nine attacks the silly argument that, even if they are not beautiful, or do not disclose truth, many works which we reject are interesting. We show that this argument is, in itself, foolish. We also show, quite briefly, that one probable reason that the argument has attained prominence is because it helps to support the many social and personal evils promoted by the princes of corporate capitalism.

We wrote this book knowing that, as Plato's repeated attacks on the sophists warn his readers, no generation will be free of sophists. Such is true of our generation, and of the twentieth century. However, in the realm of art the twentieth century is unique. During this century, in which both great and heinous events occurred, many thousands of works of sophistry invaded the realm of the visual arts, and in many instances triumphed in that realm. The immediate result of this invasion and triumph is that sophist-artists, together with sophist-critics and sophist-art-writers, have convinced museums to provide an honorable abode for many thousands of works of fakery and of sham-art. As the play, *Art*, reveals, mendacity and sophistry in art have attained respectability.

Consequently, even the casual observer discovers that many museums and galleries provide much space for works of sophistry in twentieth-century art. As we will repeatedly show in the chapters that follow, what distinguishes these works of fake art is that the so-called work of art has no relation to beauty, to truth, or to spirituality. Hence, the many rooms in museums and galleries that house these contemporary works of fake art are spiritual wastelends.

We hold that this wasteland, this undeserved triumph of sophistry should be confronted, rejected, and condemned. Plato's brilliant insights, and his relentless struggle against the sophists of his time, can serve as inspiration, and a source of encouragement in rejecting the contemporary triumphs of sophistry. Plato's dialogues and his continual struggle for truth also suggest that the challenge facing us is to confront, to reject, and to condemn the many falsehoods and the spirit of mendacity and vacuity spread by the particular sophists in our midsts.

Plato's insights, including the insight that opens this Introduction, are a source of inspiration and ecouragement because they also reveal that each generation can strive to expose the seductive deceit spread by sophists and by works of sophistry. In order to even partially succeed in such an undertaking, you must strive to discover and unveil the rare and shimmering light of truth. In this shimmering light of truth, all deceit becomes evident. It is seen as ugly, repulsive, destructive. You may even be physically repelled by it. After such an exposing of the deceit of contemporary sophistry, together with its accompanying ugliness, it is not too difficult to confront, to reject, and to condemn the writings and the many works of sophistry that prevail, including the widespread sophistry in twentieth-century art.

We believe that the following pages constitute a modest contribution to addressing this worthy challenge.

One

HEIDEGGER ON TRUTH AND ART

Martin Heidegger's essay "The Origin of the Work of Art" was first published in 1950 in German, as "Der Ursprung des Kunstwerkes." The essay is partially based on lectures that Heidegger gave on this topic at various occasions during 1935 and 1936; years later the lectures were rewritten as an essay, in preparation for publication. The fact that the essay has been available in German since 1950 and in English since 1975, is significant. Because, this profound essay, that describes the relationship of art to beauty and to truth, has been much ignored, by artists, art critics, and art historians, and also by philosophers writing on contemporary art. For instance, the writings of Arthur Danto and Jacques Barzun, cited in the Introduction, suggest that their authors have learned nothing from Heidegger's essay. We can state categorically that our broad survey of the field has revealed that this essay, and all of Heidegger's thinking on art, on truth, and on beauty has not had any discernible influence on almost all writers on art or on art criticism and art history in the second half of the twentieth century.[1]

Before briefly presenting some of the important truths found in "The Origin of the Work of Art," we wish to emphasize that what interests Heidegger, as a philosopher, is to discover, to describe, and to point to essences. In this quest, he is true to the philosophical tradition. In Plato's *The Republic*, Socrates strives to discover, to describe, and to point to the essence of justice. In Plato's *Greater Hippias*, as already mentioned, Socrates questions Hippias about the essence of beauty. In "The Origin of the Work of Art," Heidegger seeks to discover, to describe, and to point to the origin and the essence of a work of art.

At the outset, we want to disengage our discussion of Heidegger's thinking on art, from Heidegger's adherence to Nazism during the period of the Third Reich, a topic which has concerned dozens of scholars for many decades. We believe that Heidegger made an evil decision when he joined the Nazi party in 1933, and that he acted as an evil person, when he did not renounce Nazism. We also hold that he acted as an evil person when, for three decades, from 1945 until his death in 1975, he refused to recognize and to condemn the wickedness of the Nazi leaders, and of many of the German people during the Holocaust. But these evils, which we condemn and despise, do not diminish the truth that, in the twentieth century, this same wicked Martin Heidegger provided us with some of the most profound thinking concerning art that has been published.

We therefore consider it irresponsible thinking, to suggest that, because of Heidegger's links to Nazism, you can dismiss or ignore his profound insights concerning art, beauty, and spirituality. As Jean-Paul Sartre noted in the late 1940s, in a response to criticism of the links between his own thinking and that of Heidegger, if we find worthy truths in the writings of a despicable and immoral person — Sartre mentions Martin Heidegger and Jean-Jacques Rousseau — we must learn from these truths, even while rejecting the immoral person who formulated them.[2] In this book, we follow Sartre's advice.

Consequently, we find it quite sad that so many talented scholars have spent much time and energy linking Heidegger's thinking to Nazism, without addressing and learning from the important truths that appear in his writings. An example of this rather sterile approach to learning from Heidegger's essay, "The Origin of the Work of Art," is Robert Bernasconi's paper on Heidegger's essay, which he titled "The Greatness of the Work of Art." [3] Bernasconi's essay has much to do with the links between the terms that appear in Heidegger's "The Origin of the Work of Art" and terms used by the Nazis. Bernasconi also discusses Heidegger's learning from Hegel and from the Greek philosophers; he mentions other works by Heidegger in which there is some discussion of aesthetic issues, and he reviews a few other scholarly matters. But all this well-documented scholarship evades addressing Heidegger's ideas about what is genuine great art — what is its origin and essence. For instance, Bernasconi gives no example, beyond those proffered by Heidegger himself, on how Heidegger's ideas might relate to great works of art that we may encounter, say a painting by Jan Vermeer or by Edward Hopper. Not one!

Consequently, the person who wishes to learn to relate to a great work of art, say, Hopper's "Nighthawks" or one of Rembrandt's self- portraits, or Vermeer's painting that is called "View of Delft," and would like to know what Heidegger's essay suggests, learns nothing, absolutely nothing, from Bernasconi's scholarly paper. A sensitive reader might even ask himself after reading Bernasconi's paper: Has Bernasconi ever quietly stood and looked, with the concentration of his whole being, at a great original painting — say by Rembrandt, or Vermeer, or Matisse — to see if there is truth in Heidegger's essay?

Much the same is true about the discussion of "The Origin of the Work of Art" in Otto Poggeler's study *Martin Heidegger's Path of Thinking*.[4] Poggeler merely rewrites and explains many of Heidegger's difficult ideas, without ever asking if they have relevance to specific works of art that the reader may encounter.

Our sad conclusion is that within the scholarly and lay communities there is little appreciation of the valuable practical insights and provoking thoughts that emerge in "The Origin of the Work of Art." We want to stress that this lack of appreciation is evident not only among artists and critics, but even among Heidegger scholars. Hence, we have decided to present many of Heidegger's insights and thoughts that appear in this essay in an orderly manner. While briefly presenting these thoughts and insights we will, at times, relate Heidegger's thinking to great works of art and, also, to the sophistry that has emerged in some twentieth-century so-called works of art.

In the first pages of Heidegger's essay, you find the statement that the work of art is a thing among many other things in the world. In order to see what is unique in those things that are works of art, Heidegger begins by looking at the things that we encounter in the world, from the mundane to the sublime. He asks how these things are described and defined. In answer to this question, Heidegger presents and rejects three major descriptions of things that have been very prominent in Western philosophy since its inception.

The first description of a thing is that it is a substance with certain accidents. In his essay *Meditations on First Philosophy*, Descartes described himself as a thinking substance with certain qualities or accidents. Heidegger mentions that this approach to describing a thing may be problematic since it could be described as a mirroring of the sentence structure of language. In any sentence, a subject has predicates attributed to it. When I say: Van Gogh's painting of sunflowers has a yellow background, the subject or substance is Van Gogh's painting of sunflowers and the predicate or accident is the yellow background. Yet, even if viewing a thing as a substance with predicates is not confined to the mirroring of language, Heidegger rejects this description because it "does not hit upon the thingly element of the thing, its independent and self contained character."[5]

We believe that Heidegger's rejection of this description of a thing is correct, especially in relation to things which contribute to our quest for a spiritual existence, among them works of art. Consider Van Gogh's painting of sunflowers, or one of Rembrandt's self-portraits — these paintings are not merely two substances, each with its specific accidents. Such a description of these great paintings is shallow and inane. It is a manner of emasculating the spiritual power emanating from these works of art. It is an ignoring of the beauty of these paintings. Because, as Heidegger points out, the description of a great painting as a substance with accidents does not take into account the independence and the self contained character of each painting. Nor does it take into account, we would add, the beauty of each painting, a beauty which emerges in each painting in a way that expresses and is in harmony with its independence and self containment.

Another traditional philosophical description of the thing, presented by Heidegger, is "that which is perceptible by sensations in the senses belonging to sensibility."[6] During the twentieth century, such an approach was common among the promoters of behaviorism, philosophical analysis, and other schools of thought. Heidegger rejects this approach with short shrift; he explains that it does not take into account the intentional component of all perception. This intentional component is evident in every relation between my senses and things in the world.

Consider some examples. I do not hear a noise, but rather the whistle of the steamboat, or the patter of the rain on the roof. I do not smell an odor, but the pungency of the onions frying on the stove, or the sweetness of the jasmine in the garden. Such is true of all our sensations and of all the senses. Hence, Heidegger holds, a thing cannot be described as merely made up of a throng of sensations, or, as some philosophers have suggested, a bundle of sense data. Our senses already intentionally relate to the thingness of the thing to which the supposed throng of sensations belongs.

The description of a thing as made up of a throng of sensations also ignores the independence and self-containment of the thing, another reason for its being wrong. We should add that, as in the case of defining a thing as substance and accidents, describing the being of a work of art as constituted by a throng of sensations is a manner of eradicating its independence, self containment, beauty, and spirituality.

The third traditional philosophical description of a thing, mentioned by Heidegger, is that it is formed matter. Although this description of the work of art, as formed matter, prevails in almost all discussions of art, art theory, and aesthetics, Heidegger distrusts it. Before citing his reasons for this distrust it is important to point out the broad acceptance of this description of works of art. Museum tour guides, many books on art, and even the few sentences affixed beside the work of art in a museum or a gallery — almost always these manners of presenting art to the viewer relate to the work of art as formed matter. Furthermore, Heidegger adds, "Form and content are the most hackneyed concepts under which anything and everything may be subsumed."[7]

The reason Heidegger distrusts relating to the work of art as formed matter is that this view is adopted from our manner of relating to the equipment that we use. Human beings create tools and equipment by giving specific forms to certain pieces of matter. Shoemakers give the form of a shoe to the pieces of leather that they sew, bind, and glue together. Chip-makers create a specific form for passing on information on the thin piece of silicon that will be installed in the personal computer. Potters give the form of a jug to the lump of clay that each potter molds. What characterizes a piece of equipment is that it is made for something, fore employment and use.

Both the granite boulder in a remote valley and the work of art are not equipment. The jug may be self-contained like the boulder, but the shape of the jug was determined by the potter. No person determined the form of the boulder. The work of art was also created and determined by a human being, but it has a self-sufficient presence that the piece of equipment lacks. A portrait by Rembrandt, Verdi's opera *Aida*, Michelangelo's sculpture of David are great works of art whose self-sufficient presence is immediately evident. No pair of shoes, no silicon chip, no simple clay jug, nor any other piece of equipment that we daily use has the self-sufficient presence of a great work of art.

At this point we wish to add that a piece of equipment, say a pair of shoes, may be pretty, or cute, or aestheticly appealing, or perhaps even handsome or lovely. But, a pair of shoes will never be beautiful, in the Heideggerian sense of the word beautiful, which we accept. For the simple reason that the term "beautiful" does not apply to any piece of equipment. Why? Heidegger answers later in the essay, especially when he describes what constitutes the beautiful, and its firm links to the unconcealing of truth. We can here mention that the piece of equipment does not unconceal truth. We present Heidegger's description of the beautiful later in this chapter. At this point, however, he has made clear that it is wrong to describe the great work of art as merely formed matter. Such a shallow description of the work of art ignores, among other things, the fact that great art has a self-sufficient presence, and that great art is beautiful.

The three traditional philosophical descriptions of things that Heidegger rejected have entered into various combinations, which may be skipped. We have already seen that the problem with these descriptions of things is that they often shackle and restrain our thinking about the essence of a specific thing, in this case, the work of art. Heidegger holds that they also shackle and restrain our thinking about the character of a mere thing, say a boulder, and about the character of a piece of equipment. To see the essence of a thing, he suggests, we must let it be in its being, and not try to fit it into a preconceived model of thinking.

To learn to see the essence of a thing, Heidegger suggests that we consider a piece of equipment, say, a pair of a peasant woman's shoes. Put differently, by looking at a pair of shoes, Heidegger wants to grasp what is the essence of the piece of equipment. We can consider such shoes, he suggests, in a painting by Vincent Van Gogh. We all know what shoes are for, they clothe our feet. We also know that the matter and the form of a pair of shoes will differ in accordance with the use to which they are to be put. Shoes to dance ballet differ from shoes for field work, and they both differ from boots for mountain climbing. In the process of using the pair of shoes, we encounter its specific character as equipment. But if that is so, the great painting of a pair of shoes reveals the character of these specific shoes, and thus opens us to an entire way of life. In the case of the peasant woman's shoes in Van Gogh's painting,

> the toilsome tread of the worker stares forth. In the stiffly rugged heaviness of the shoes there is the accumulated tenacity of her [the peasant woman's] slow trudge through the far-spreading and ever-uniform furrows of the field swept by a raw wind. Under the soles slides the loneliness of the field-path as evening falls. In the shoes vibrates the silent call of the earth, its quiet gift of the

ripening grain and its unexplained self-refusal in the
fallow desolation of the wintry field.[8]

With such eloquent prose, Heidegger continues to reveal the world of
he peasant woman, a world of which we may become aware when we look
carefully at Van Gogh's beautiful painting of her shoes. Heidegger's goal is to
enlighten us as to how Van Gogh's painting of the peasant woman's shoes, of
this simple, usable, reliable equipment with which she clothes her feet, opens
us to the daily life and the world of a peasant woman. Thus, Heidegger states,
"The art work let us know what shoes are in truth."[9]

We purposely do not discuss the stupid attempt by Meyer Schapiro to
prove that the shoes in Van Gogh's painting do not belong to a peasant
woman, but rather to the painter.[10] Even if such is true, it has nothing to do
with the truth that Heidegger unconceals concerning the essence of equipment.
Schapiro's vacuous scholarship has strangled his own ability to think about the
ideas that Heidegger presents about the essence of art. In what follows, we
shall accept Heidegger's statement concerning Van Gogh's painting as valid,
because we wish to learn from Heidegger's ideas. The validity of these ideas
has no relationship to who wore the shoes that Van Gogh painted.

Consider, for a moment, some of the immediate outcomes of Heidegger's
statement. The truth of the peasant woman's pair of shoes, and with it the
Being-in-the-world of the peasant woman, have become unconcealed in Van
Gogh's painting. Heidegger generalizes from this example and remarks that
great works of art very frequently unconceal major truths about beings; among
the truths about beings that great works of art unconceal, he includes truths
about pieces of equipment and about many other aspects of human existence in
the world. Rembrandt's beautiful self-portraits, for instance, unconceal truths
about his own personality and about his Being-in-the-world. Some of Balthus's
beautiful paintings unconceal truths about the delightful innocence of nudity;
yet, you will also find beautiful paintings by Balthus which unconceal truths
about the sordid links between seductive eroticism and alienation in our
everyday life.

In passing, we can point out that no such major truth about beings becomes
unconcealed in an abstract painting by Piet Mondrian or by Vasili Kandinsky,
or by Mark Rothko, or by Jackson Pollock. Nor does a major truth about
beings or about human existence become unconcealed in the painting of an
American flag or a target by Jasper Johns, or in the painting of a can of
Campbell's Soup by Andy Warhol. Nor does a major truth emerge in the
Minimalist white painting that Serge purchased in the play, *Art*. Is it not an act
of sophistry, to call these paintings works of art?

Heidegger is aware that his statement concerning the link between the
work of art and truth may be considered problematic. One reason is that art has
usually been considered to be beautiful, or to belong to the realm of the
aesthetic. Hence, an important question emerges. What is the link between

beauty and truth? This seemingly simple question requires an examination of both basic concepts: beauty and truth.

Heidegger immediately points out that the accepted concept of truth is not very appropriate to a work of art. If, as is currently held by many thinkers and scientists, truth is merely the agreement of a statement with a fact, or with a state of affairs, then this concept of truth has nothing to do with the work of art. This accepted concept of truth, however, is quite appropriate when we discuss mere things or pieces of equipment. At this point, disturbing questions emerge. For instance: Do we need a special concept of truth to relate to the work of art? And, if so, what concept of truth may we use to relate to a work of art?

In response to these and to other similarly disturbing questions, Heidegger decides to examine in depth the relationship between a work of art and truth. He clearly states that the great work of art discloses to us something essential about the Being of beings. But to better understand this important disclosure, Heidegger recognizes that he must once again turn to the task of examining what is the essence and the origin of the work of art. Once this essence and this origin are made clear, he indicates, we will have gained a better understanding of the relation between the work of art and truth.

From his presentation of previous unsuccessful attempts, by thinkers in past centuries, to understand the thingly aspect of the work of art, Heidegger concludes that these attempts overlooked the self-subsistence of the work. But this self-subsistence is often severely limited or even partially destroyed when a work is torn out of its historical context and presented to the public, say when the portrait hangs in a museum. Still, in great works of art, as in Van Gogh's painting of the peasant woman's shoes, or in Rembrandt's self portraits, or in Michelangelo's sculpture "David," or in Vermeer's "View of Delft," even after the work has been torn out of its natural or historical context, remnants of the self-subsistence are retained. Hence, we can encounter a realm that is opened up to us by the work of art.

Heidegger has already suggested that this opening up of a realm, a world, is the truth at work in the work of art. In order to better comprehend this opening up of a realm by the work of art, and to show the truth at work in the work of art, Heidegger decides to consider a work of art that is not representational. He decides to look at a Greek temple. He asks: How does this Greek temple, standing there in the rock-cleft valley, open up truth in a realm, a world? Heidegger's answer is:

> It is the temple-work that first fits together and at the same time gathers around itself the unity of those paths and relations in which birth and death, disaster and blessing, victory and disgrace, endurance and decline acquire the shape of destiny for human being.[11]

Thus, for the community of people who frequented the Greek temple in the valley, who prayed there and gathered there for their communal celebrations and days of sadness, the temple was a sanctuary where they could relate to their gods. But it was also the meeting place of many personal paths and relations that existed in their community, and characterized the community. In addition, the temple was often the meeting place of the paths of the entire community's choices, and hence, of its destiny in the world. As such, the temple opened up the world of history and destiny for the persons and for the members of the Greek community who frequented it.

Heidegger is suggesting that when a work of architecture is beautiful, it becomes a meeting place for the paths of the personal and communal choices of the persons and the community who live in its immediate vicinity and who come regularly to the building. Only then will the building serve to open up the world of history and destiny for that community, and for its members. This opening up of the world of history and destiny discloses many of the truths in the life of the specific community which relates to the work of architecture. Hence, the beauty of a work of architecture as a work of art, in this case a Greek temple standing in a rock-cleft vally, is again linked to truth.

We wish to mention another point in which Heidegger's thinking is correct. Little is left of the beauty and truth of the Greek temple if it is torn out of its place in the valley, and in the history of a specific community, and transferred to a museum — one such Greek temple has been set up in a large hall inside the British Museum in London. A remnant of the beauty of this Greek temple may haunt the temple and the museum visitor may sense this beauty, but its relation to truth is hollow. Nothing of the throbbing life and the destiny of a Greek community emanates from this large museum piece. Heidegger might have added that the temple in the museum no longer discloses the truths that engaged the community that it served; hence it presents only a very faded beauty, if at all.

If, as we believe, there is much truth in Heidegger's thinking, it has relevance for many fields of architecture. For instance, the pyramids in Egypt, and especially the three gigantic Giza pyramids near Cairo, can be termed colossal and awesome. However, they are not worthy architecture; nor are the pyramids beautiful. The reason is simple. Each pyramid was built by tens of thousands of suffering slaves working for years so as to establish a monument in which there would be preserved the mummified body of one Pharaoh. As such, these mammoth monuments of gigantic hewn boulders, which were built solely so as to mark and to preserve the tomb room of one Pharaoh, have almost no personal relation to the ancient Egyptian's daily life. The pyramids never were built so as to be a meeting place of a living community, in which simple people may grapple with their personal and communal history and destiny, and with the truths of their existence.

The result is evident to any visitor at Giza. These colossal, rock-built geometric forms stand there towering over you in the desert; you soon sense that they are gigantic monuments of alienation, huge instruments made of hewn rocks, with no truth to convey. Hence, they cannot open up the world of history and of destiny for the Egyptian community today. Moreover, we do not believe that the three pyramids of Giza ever could be a meeting place for the members of a living community. Because Heidegger's criterion is valid. The pyramids do not open up a world, they do not relate to the major truths of the ancient Egyptian's daily existence. At most, they are perverse expressions of political power, quite similar to Nero's fiddling while he witnessed the burning of Rome.

Much the same can be said of many ancient Egyptian monumental sculptures, including the Sphinx. We also mean the giant stone sculptures of different Pharaohs and gods, prominent among them are those sculptures of Ramses II. Almost all of these works, many of which can be found in the Cairo Museum, and which we carefully scrutinized on many visits to Egypt, are totally alienated from the person who encounters them. The viewer of these monumental sculptures, or of the Sphinx, does not encounter these works as opening up a world in which beauty and truth are valued. If they hint as to the life of the ancient Egyptians, they convince us that this life lacked spirituality. It is, therefore, quite impossible to imagine these monumental sculptures opening up a world, or presenting a worthy truth, to the members of the ancient Egyptian community.

Our statements concerning the pyramids do not at all accord with the accepted approach of many writers on the history of art. Hence, let us attempt to be vivid. Can you imagine the 100,000 slaves who worked daily for thirty years to build the Great Pyramid for the mummy of the not-yet dead Cheops? If you can, would you dare to suggest that these slaves can relate to the outcome of their harsh toil, cruel drudgery, and personal exploitation as opening up a world for them? Of course not!

Nor can we believe that the Cheops Pyramid opened up a world for the thousands of Egyptian slave-drivers and overseers of the 100,000 slaves who daily pushed each boulder from the Nile to the site of the pyramid and then up the hill to its specific place in the pyramid structure; the wheel was not used when building the pyramid. Nor did the pyramid open a world for the engineers and for the priests who oversaw the work. The same may be said of the slaves, the builders, and the overseers of the Sphinx and of the other monumental sculptures, such as those of Ramses II. For today's viewer of all these works, it is evident that in them no truth concerning human existence becomes unconcealed when encountering these colossal works. It is also evident that no beauty emerges from these monstrous constructions that remain from ancient Egypt. Nothing worthy appeals to the person who meets them. They seem to be colossal, sterile, and perverse expressions of a barren and bizarre culture.

The Hebrew Bible, which rejects all idols, vehemently rejects the ancient Egyptian culture and religion as based on idolatry, and hence lacking genuine spirituality. We would add that there exist gigantic testimonies to this lack of genuine spirituality in the life and culture of ancient Egypt: the pyramids, the Sphinx, and the many monumental sculptures of the Pharaohs. We could also, in all humility, suggest that these gigantic testimonies of Egyptian culture are quite perverse. After all, building the Great Pyramid to house the corpse of one Pharaoh, Cheops, is not a normal expression of grandeur, or of morality, or of truth, or of beauty. Put succinctly, such a grandiose endeavor as the Great Pyramid is perverse since it is quite evident that this cultural expression of ancient Egypt is not beautiful, not spiritual, and did not open a realm of truth for the Egyptian community. We conclude that even if the pyramids, the sphinx, and the monumental sculptures of Pharaohs are bold and gigantic expressions of trends in Egyptian culture, they are not worthy works of art.

At this point, four poignant questions concerning contemporary art may emerge. The questions are based on the insight that the pyramids, the Sphinx, and the monumental sculptures of ancient Egypt are unspiritual, not beautiful, and do not open a realm of truth.

The questions are: Could not conclusions similar to those that we reached about these unspiritual cultural expressions of ancient Egypt apply to Andy Warhol's paintings of a can of Campbell's Soup, or to Jean Dubuffet's installation of a "Cave" that is exhibited in the Georges Pompidou Center for Culture and Modern Art in Paris? Could we not compare the lack of truth, beauty, and spirituality of the Egyptian pyramids to Warhol's can of soup, to Jasper John's painting of a flag, or to the monumental installations, and other weird works of so-called art, including Dubuffet's installations, that have proliferated lately in many museums, and near the headquarters of many corporate capitalist firms? Should we not conclude that these unbeautiful, anti-spiritual, bizarre, and alienated so-called works of art express certain perverse trends in contemporary culture? Finally, would it be correct to firmly state that these perverse expressions of contemporary culture are not worthy works of art?

The answer emerging from Heidegger's thinking on the origin of the work of art to each of these four questions is a resounding: Yes!

To be a beautiful work of art, Heidegger believes, means to set up a world. In that world, truth is unconcealed. The work of art sets up the world with the simple materials of what Heidegger calls Earth. Colors, stone, wood, hues, words, tones, and many other components are all included in what he calls the Earth.

But, what is a world? It is definitely not a mere collection of all the beings that we may encounter in the universe, from quarks and genomes, through persons and Van Gogh's paintings, to planets, galaxies, and black holes. A world transcends the mere collection of beings that we believe constitute it. A world is not an object, and the existence of a world is unique to human beings. Animals and plants live in an environment. Only human beings establish a world, and live in it.

World, let us say again, is not an object among other objects. It is linked to a way of being. Heidegger's formulation, that explains what he terms world, is difficult but illuminating. He writes: "World is the ever non-objective to which we are subject as long as the paths of birth and death, blessing and curse keep us transported in Being."[12] Heidegger adds that the world comes into being for us human beings only where decisions are made concerning our history and which relate to our very Being. A stone, or plants and animals, do not make decisions concerning their history and Being, hence they have no world.

Underlying both of Heidegger's formulations is the simple fact that the mode of existence of the human entity links Being and time. It is, therefore, not surprising that he called his major philosophical work *Being and Time*. Recognizing the fact that it was born and that it will die, is unique to Dasein, the human entity; this recognition is one of the most fundamental ways that a person links his or her Being to time. This linking of Being and time is, Heidegger believes, the foundation of the world that the person establishes. Because of this foundation, the human entity can relate to Being through involvement in the world, which means involvement with the beings that exist in the present, have existed in the past, or will exist in the future.

Consequently, as long as a person relates to the past, to the present, and to the future, by this relating the person is transported in Being. By the term "transported in Being," we take Heidegger to mean living in time and recognizing that we live in time. Only by such a recognition can an entity be transported in Being and recognize oneself as transported. A stone, a plant, and an animal do not relate to time and hence are quite fixed in their being. They are not transported in Being. Only the human being is transported in Being, and by this way of existing, a world which is non-objective comes into being. By the term "non-objective," Heidegger means that this world is not only constituted by a group of objects and external relations between these objects. Heidegger's formulation emphasizes meaningful events, such as birth and death, blessing and curse, which are central to a person's relation to time and to Being. These events are recognized and related to by human beings, who also recognize that they are transported in Being.

Essential to the genuine work of art is that it sets up a world, and opens it to the persons who relate to the work. For such to occur, the materials of Earth used in the work must come into the Open created by the work's world. For instance, the redness of the roof shingles and the reflections in the water of the stream in Vermeer's beautiful painting, "View of Delft," helps to open, for the person who looks at the painting, the world of the residents of Delft. This world includes the view of the city of Delft from the vantage point beyond the river where Vermeer stood and painted. This opening of a world occurs, because, as Heidegger puts it, the redness of the shingles shines forth and discloses the beauty that can be found in the human blending of simple building materials, when looked at from a unique perspective. The redness shines forth in its uniqueness, and its shining blends harmoniously with the shining forth of all the other earthly aspects of the world portrayed in the painting, say, the reflections in the water. Consequently, when looking at the painting, these red roofs are revealed in their earthly qualities, while being part of the world that has been opened in Vermeer's painting.

Similarly, the authoritative, warning, deep-bass voice of the dead Commendatore of Seville, heard from offstage, in the graveyard scene near the end of Mozart's opera, *Don Juan*, rings forth. This deep-bass voice, blending with the other background music that rings forth, helps open the person who is listening to the opera to the conflict between the quest of unbridled seduction of women, that informs Don Juan's being, and the world of Christianity, with its firm belief in sin and retribution. You might even say that the ringing deep-bass voice of the Commendatore is a religious-ethical response — from beyond the world, but based in the world — to Don Juan's evil dedication to continual sensual and sexual seduction of women. The earthliness of the Commenda-tore's voice is rooted in those tones of the human voice that can be used to condemn evil, to demand retribution and justice, and to mete out punishment for evil deeds.

Heidegger's understanding of the role of the elements of Earth in the origin of a work of art is significant to grasping the profundity of his thinking on art. It also discloses additional aspects of the poverty of much contemporary art, for instance, pop-art and conceptual art, in which there is no conflict between Earth and the opening up of a world. We return to this point when discussing the so-called sculptures by Carl Andre in the next chapter.

Heidegger points out that any attempt to scientifically analyze or to discover the rational makeup of an element of Earth is bound to fail. The soundwaves that are the accepted physical description of the Commendatore's voice tell us nothing about the musical impression made by this deep-bass voice. The soundwaves disclose nothing that can tell us why these tones and notes are appropriate to condemn and to threaten Don Juan, and to notify him that retribution for his sins will come shortly. Similarly, the specific waves of light, that conventional physical science tells us constitute the red of the roofs of Delft in Vermeer's painting, disclose nothing about the city of Delft and the beauty of the view and of the world opened up by the painting.

Consequently, Heidegger reaches an important conclusion. Elements of the Earth appear as themselves — again, think of the red roofs of Delft in Vermeer's painting, and the deep-bass voice of the Commendatore — only when they are perceived as self sufficient, and as shrinking from disclosure by rational and other means. The rose is a rose is a rose, as Gertrude Stein once put it, in an enlightening statement from which much can be learned, and which we will cite again. Indeed, the rose as a rose defies analysis and rational reduction, say, into light waves, specific odors, and the like. Learning from Heidegger, we can state that like other elements of Earth, the rose is self-sufficient. And, as self-sufficient, the rose shrinks from disclosure and analysis. In great works of plastic art, the elements of the Earth shine forth, yet they are self-sufficient and shrink from disclosure.

All this is important because, in relating to a work of art, we must direct our being to see the work as it stands there confronting us, or to listen to the musical composition as it is heard. To relate to a great work of art as disclosing a world, we must refrain from analysing and from explaining what we see or what we hear. Instead, we must learn to respect the work of art and to relate to its self-sufficiency, a self-sufficiency that cannot be analyzed, reduced, or explained away. We must learn to accept the fact that the work of art shrinks from disclosure. If we follow such a path, a humble knowledge of our own limitations when confronting great works of art may slowly emerge. We will learn that we will never be able to disclose what makes Vermeer's painting, "View of Delft," so beautiful. We will discover that we will never be able to fully articulate the truths opened up in Rembrandt's magnificent self-portraits. We hold that this knowing that we do not know is similar to Socrates' wisdom.

Pop-Art, such as the enlarged comics strips of Roy Lichtenstein, have no self-sufficiency. These two-dimensional enlarged comics strips purport to arouse the viewer's curiosity and passing interest. Many viewers merely wish to understand and unravel what the works of Lichtenstein seemingly represent or suggest. Hung on the wall, as if they were a work of respectable art, the comics strips are a weird puzzle for the lay visiter to a museum. They hang their without beauty, with no truth, and with no self-sufficiency, solely dependent upon the curiosity or the interest of the viewer. If we attempt to scrutinize them, say, in accordance with the guidence we have gleaned from Heidegger's essay, we easily discover the following facts. These oversized comics strips are definitely not beautiful — no one has ever proffered such a suggestion. Nor do they convey any worthy truth about the Being of beings. Nor do they open a world. In short, they are works of sophistry, they attempt to attribute the being of art to works that are not art.

What does happen? Lichtenstein's enlarged comics strips hang there on the wall of a museum, arousing curiosity, ambiguous in their very Being, and serving as a topic for idle talk. Learning from Heidegger's ontological masterpiece, *Being and Time*, we can categorically state that Lichtenstein's comic strips cannot and do not relate to the authentic person. Quite the opposite is the case. These large pictures of trivia, that masquerade as art, are disclosed primarily to the unique being whom Heidegger states is the author of human inauthenticity: the "They."[13] Developing this theme, however, would, at present take us astray. Yet support of the theme emerges throughout this book.

We emphasize that Lichtenstein's enlarged comics strips are works of sophistry. Is it not evident that these enlarged comics strips are fakes and not art, since they are artifacts that have no truth to convey, are not beautiful, and seem to scoff at spirituality? Is there any essential difference between these art, since they are artifacts that have no truth to convey, are not beautiful, and seem to scoff at spirituality? Is there any essential difference between these works of sophistry and the works of Minimalist and Conceptualist art? Are not paintings, such as Warhol's cans of Campbell's Soup, and Mondrian's 1921 "Composition with Red, Yellow, and Blue" also fake art? If we accept Heidegger's insights and ideas, is it not appropriate to call these museum pieces: trivia masquerading as art? Is it not true, that such works of sophistry, like Lichtenstein's enlarged comics strips, Warhol's cans of soup, and Mondrian's abstract compositions also ruin human spirituality? Our answer to all the questions is: Yes.

Heidegger points to the unique relation between world and Earth in the being of the work of art. The great work of art unites in its being the setting up of a world, and, with it, the setting forth of Earth in a manner that its unique elements can shine forth. In such a great work, there is not a blending of world and of Earth, but a tension between these two major constituents of the work of art. The reason for this tension is that the world opened up by a work of art discloses some of the paths chosen by a historical people. In contrast to this opening up of paths, the elements of Earth in the work of art are self-secluding, sheltering, and concealing. The tension exists between the opening up of a world which the work of great art presents, and the self-secluding and concealing of the elements of the Earth in that same work of art.

In order to better comprehend Heidegger's thoughts, consider the following examples of twentieth-century works of great art created in the United States: the poetry of Robert Frost, the drama of Tennessee Williams, the paintings of Edward Hopper, the music of George Gershwin, the buildings planned by Frank Lloyd Wright, the photography of Alfred Stieglitz, the novels of William Faulkner. It is not difficult to perceive that all of these twentieth-century beautiful works of art disclose significant truths about some of the paths chosen by some of the people of the United States. Each of these works of art thus opens up the world of the people of the United States.

We will only discuss two examples from the above list, which will partially reveal the tension that Heidegger describes between the opening up of a world and the elements of the Earth. The first example is the drama of Tennessee Williams, which discloses truths about the evil and perverse paths of life chosen by many people in the deep South of the United States, especially in states such as Louisiana and Mississippi. An element of Earth that we repeatedly hear in the plays of Tennessee Williams is the deep southern drawl, blended with a sweet over-politeness. This southern drawl rings out; it helps to open up, for the spectator in the theatre, the world of the deep South in the United States. Tennessee Williams's plays also reveal that this sweet-polite southern drawl is also a subtle manner of concealing truths. More, this truth-concealing drawl both conceals and expresses the decadence, the degradation, the perverse relationships, and the sanctioning of evil that characterized life in

Furthermore, for any other speaker of English, hearing the southern drawl means being faced with a regional accent of English that is self-secluding, sheltering, and concealing. Much of the meaning and nuances of what is said in this drawl may elude the non-southern English speaker. Hence, we are faced with the tension between the opening of a world to the spectator in which the southern drawl is a component, and the concealing of truths and self-seclusion of elements of that world by the same southern drawl. A compelling character, who, with her sweet and polite deep southern drawl, forcefully conveys the tension that exists between opening up the world of the deep South, and the concealing of truths about some of its profound evils and perversity, is Blanche DuBois in Tennessee Williams's play, *A Streetcar Named Desire.*[14]

Similarly, consider the jazz melodies that are central to George Gershwin's concert music. These melodies open up, for the listener to classical music, a realm of music that partially expresses the world and the life of African-Americans in the United States. Recall, for instance, the song "I've Got Plenty of Nothing," which is sung in Gershwin's opera *Porgy and Bess.* For decades, the musical creativity expressed in jazz had been confined to popular music; jazz flourished in bars and popular concert halls. Gershwin's genius was in hearing the beauty of these melodies and in blendng some of them into various orchestra and vocal concert pieces that partially open up the world of the African-Americans. In his beautiful concert music, the jazz melodies of this African-American world ring out and appeal to the listener.

But tension between the world and Earth also emerges in Gershwin's music. One reason is that, in Gershwin's classical compositions, jazz melodies become ordered and final; these ordered jazz melodies shelter and conceal the uniqueness of jazz as a spontaneous and, often, group-musical-creation which is continually being created and recast by the musicians during its presentation. By concealing the musical spontaneity and creativity that is central to genuine jazz, Gershwin's compositions also shelter and conceal many spontaneous melodious elements of the life of the African-Americans that the jazz melodies have partially opened up.

Another reason for tension between opening up a world and the elements of Earth is the non-conventional use of certain musical instruments in Gershwin's classical compositions, say, the non-conventional opening notes of "Rhapsody in Blue," that are played by a saxaphone. These haunting notes of "Rhapsody in Blue" ring out; they immediately appeal to the listener, and present a musical theme that will continually emerge throughout the composition. The notes, and their being played by the saxaphone, also partially express musical themes and modes of musical expression created and explored by African-Americans as they traversed their historical paths of life in the United States. But these same haunting and beautiful notes, only hint as to the substance, and yes, the great suffering that has characterized the African-American paths of life in the United States. At best, the melody played by the saxaphone gives the listener an inkling of the African-American search for self-expression in a white, European, hostile, enslaving society. Hence, the haunting and appealing opening notes played by the saxaphone in "Rhapsody in Blue," also conceal and shelter the African-American paths of life from its listeners.

Heidegger explains that the tension in a great work of art, between the opening up of a world and the elements of Earth, should not be viewed as opposition. It is a striving, in which opponents raise each other to new levels by surrendering to the hidden source of their being. Consider the hidden source of the being of the polite southern drawl of the deep South, say, as expressed in the plays of Tennessee Williams. This deep southern drawl, in its being, is a manner of concealing from all speakers and listeners the many crimes of racism against African-Americans that prevailed for centuries in the deep South of the United States. These crimes, and the racism which justified them, created great suffering for African-Americans and also ruined the souls of the white oppressors and racists. One way chosen by the white oppressors of concealing this ruin was by always speaking politely and with a sweet drawl. Of course, the southern drawl can be linked to other aspects of life in the deep South, including the climate, the society, the history. But it helped to conceal the prominent evils of racism.

The tension that this deep southern drawl creates in the plays of Tennessee Williams, say, in *A Streetcar Named Desire*, helps raise the play to a spiritual level. The play is raised to this level by subtlely surrendering to the spectator one of the hidden sources of the being of the polite southern drawl, which is perfectly articulated by Blanche Dubois. As the play ends, the spectator is well aware that her perfect southern drawl was a manner by which Blanche endeavors to conceal the devastation and the evil that characterizes her being, and much of her society.

Heidegger adds that great works of art instigate such a striving between the opening up of a world and the elements of the Earth. There seems to be a battle between these two trends in the great work of art. This striving, and battle, he adds, raises the work to new levels, thus disclosing new truths about beings, and perhaps even about Being. However, a question emerge. How does this disclosing of truth come about in work of art — in the midst of the tension and the battle between the world opened up and the elements of Earth? Even partially answering this question will lead to many new thoughts concerning the work of art, and hence it requires a new chapter.

Before turning to that question in Chapter Three, we dedicate a short chapter to an ontological fact: the human being longs for truth and for beauty. We believe that this important fact is ignored by many of the producers of twentieth-century fake art, and their supporters.

In closing this chapter, we can state categorically that, in the works of fake art that abound in museums and galleries, including these works that we have mentioned and condemned, no such tension as that described by

Heidegger exists between world and Earth. In a citation from Francis Bacon, which we cite at the end of Chapter Five, he recognizes and condemns the lack of tension in all Minimalist paintings. We go further. It is not only in Minimalist painting that tension is lacking. In the flags and targets painted by Jasper Johns, or in the abstract paintings of Vasili Kandinsky, or in the abstract or gestural expressionist pieces drip-painted by Jackson Pollock, or in the childlike semi-surrealist paintings and installations produced by Joan Miro, no world is opened up. In these so-called works of art, only elements of the Earth are exhibited. Hence, in works of fake art, such as Serge's white painting in *Art*, or a drip-painting by Jackson Pollock, no tension can occur between the elements of Earth and a world that has been opened up. Furthermore, no truths about beings can be discerned in these vacuous works of sophistry.

Need we add, that these works of fake art are — even for the lay viewer who has *not* been told that they are important pieces of art — quite frequently ugly?

Two

THE LONGING FOR TRUTH AND BEAUTY

Before presenting additional illuminating ideas found in "The Origin of the Work of Art," we believe that an underlying ontological fact that is central to Heidegger's thinking must be emphasized and, at least partially, clarified. The ontological fact, which can already be found in the thinking of Socrates and Plato, is that human beings have a longing for truth and for beauty. In his essay, Heidegger assumes implicitly that great art appeals to this human longing for truth and for beauty. From our extensive reading of his other writings and lectures, we have learned that Heidegger believes that the longing and search for truth is central to the Being of every free authentic person. This longing and search is also crucial for thinking. Probably one reason that such a longing emerged among humans is that only human beings live with language and relate to the world with that language. Hence, only human beings can question and unconceal, albeit partially, truths about the Being of beings.

Other philosophers have repeatedly indicated that the longing for truth and for beauty makes persons unique among all the beings in the world. Some religious philosophers — Nicolas Berdyaev, whom we discuss later in this study, comes to mind — have even argued that this longing for truth and for beauty is what places human beings on a higher rung than the angels, who experience no such longing.

Unfortunately, precisely this human longing for truth and for beauty is rejected by almost all of the producers of twentieth-century works of fake art, often with scorn and derision. Why? One obvious answer is that these producers of fake art know that their so-called works of art do not relate to or respond to the longing for truth and for beauty. This rejection of the longing for truth and for beauty in the works of fake art needs to be made more explicit.

At the end of Chapter One, we pointed to a way, emerging from Heidegger's thinking, of distinguishing between works of fake art and works of genuine art. Only the work of genuine art opens up a world and establishes a tension between that opened world and the elements of Earth that express the work of art. This tension is necessary for the work of art to be able to proffer both beauty and truth to the viewer of the work of visual art, or to the listener to the musical or poetic work of art.

A vivid example of such tension can be seen in the beautiful sculptures of Auguste Rodin. In his bronze sculptures, say "The Thinker" or "Balzac," the bronze is rigid and inflexible, it reveals its metallic qualities; in contrast, both sculptures unconceal truths about the throbbing dynamics of human life, with its dimension of spirituality. No such tension exists in the works of sophistry in twentieth-century art. We believe that one major reason for this lack of tension is that these works of sophistry do not open up a world.

Like the canvass painted totally white in the play *Art*, works of fake art frequently feature the mere display of elements of Earth, without opening up a world. Hence these works do not establish the tension necessary for beauty and for truth to be present in the work of art. Unfortunately, in the twentieth century, such a mere displaying of elements of Earth became widespread in both painting and sculpture. These uninspiring displays of works of fake art, which are based on a mere displaying of elements of Earth, are often given much space in museums and galleries. Furthermore, these instances of sophistry in twentieth-century art are frequently crowned with bouquets of accolades in the mainstream corporate capitalist press; they are also usually praised in publications or media broadcasts dedicated to art.

Consider Carl Andre, a contemporary American who announces that he is a sculptor. Andre's so-called art, which has been broadly exhibited, consists in erecting brick walls, or producing identical modules of red cedar blocks, or of tin, or of other pieces of ordinary material. Andre's walls and modules merely stand there in the galleries and museums where they are exhibited, taking up much space.

On 22 July 2000, a full page essay on Carl Andre and the works of so-called art that he produces and exhibits was published in *The Economist*.

The essay was written in honor of an exhibit of his works that had opened at the Whitechapel Gallery in London. The essay included a laudatory description of Carl Andre's work, and brief inserts from an interview with Andre. Here is a telling citation.

> Mr Andre's works often consist of identical modules, in linear or square configurations, fashioned from ordinary materials, unattached to each other, unpainted and unadorned... "What I wanted was a sculpture free of human association," explains Mr Andre, "a sculpture which would allow matter to speak for itself, something almost neolithic. I am essentially not a Minimalist,... but a Matterist. My work celebrates the property of matter, whether it be red cedar, tin or bismuth." Mr Andre doesn't transform his materials. He presents them. His work represents a life long love affair with matter.

We mention, only in passing, the fact that it is impossible to create "a sculpture free of human association," as Andre holds. Wherever a sculpture stands, in a gallery, an atelier, a museum, a room, or a street, persons relate to it, associate with it, and relate it to their situation, to their intentions, to their Being-in-the-world. Furthermore, as indicated in Chapter One, the entire concept of "matter" is a human determination. "Matter" is an abstraction that has little to do with the entities that we encounter in the world, and especially in the realm of art. In the world, we encounter this lemon, and not a small, round, yellow, sour, piece of "matter."

Furthermore, ants, eagles, and other members of the animal world do not think about or discuss "matter," or relate to "matter," since matter does not "speak for itself." Matter is a human concept, and that concept is part of human language and of the way persons establish a world and speak about that world in which they exist and interact. Consequently, "celebrating the properties of matter," whatever that obscure phrase may mean, is a human endeavor, a human way of relating to beings, of associating with beings.

In short, Andre's remarks, that supposedly justify his endeavors, about "a sculpture free of human association," are mistaken, unfounded, and vacuous. They are inane and inconsistent with human existence. We suspect that Andre's inanities and inconsistencies are mere attempts to camouflage his continual presentation of works that are fake art, works that do not relate to the human longing for beauty and for truth. Thus, his use of the concept "neolithic" to describe his brick walls or tin modules is weird, at best. As noted, we call such irresponsible use of concepts: sophistry. It is hardly surprising that Andre's attempts to justify his frivolous fake art is based on sophistry.

Andre's brick walls and modules of red cedar or tin are examples of fake art because, in his so-called sculptures, Andre is trying to eliminate the tension that must exist, in any work of art, between world and Earth. In Heidegger's terms, Andre's so-called sculptures attempt to display elements of Earth, without opening up a world, and hence without engaging in the challenge of creating a genuine work of art. Consequently, the modules that he presents will never establish the tension between world and Earth needed for beauty to emerge and for truth to become unconcealed.

Unfortunately, Andre is not alone in exhibiting such modules of "matter" and calling them works of art. What is more, foolish statements and weird stupidities, that are similar to Andre's inconsistent and superficial declarations, are hardly rare. Such unfounded statements and stupidities are repeatedly announced and broadly accepted by journalists who write on art shows, by some historians of art, and by those contemporary critics and other sophists, who, for decades, have supported the many works of sophistry in twentieth-century art. We will present additional examples of such writing throughout this book.

The rejection of the human longing for beauty and for truth is mild in the above citation that was taken from the essay about Andre, who ignores beauty and truth. Indeed, for the visitor of the gallery, it is not difficult to discern that Andre's brick walls, tin modules, and other productions have no relationship to beauty and to truth.

For an additional example from the many works of fake art that ignore the human longing for beauty and for truth, consider the large drip-painted canvasses of Jackson Pollock. When he engaged in drip-painting his large canvasses of so-called Abstract Expressionism, Pollock evidently didn't care a hoot about truth or about beauty. At least, he never suggested that he cared about truth and beauty. Furthermore, the many critics and intellectuals, who enthusiastically support the works of Pollock, and other works of sophistry in twentieth-century art that are exhibited in thousands of galleries and museums around the world, dismiss this longing for truth and for beauty as irrelevant to art.

Here is a bizarre philosophical instance of the dismissal of the human longing for beauty and for truth when discussing twentieth-century art. The well known art historian, who specializes in the history of painting and sculpture, Herbert Read, holds that the philosophy of modern art defines art in a "positive and decisive manner. This philosophy defines art as a means of conceiving the world *visually*."[1]

Without trying to fathom Read's weird definition, or the jumbled explanation that he presents so as to justify this definition, we can see that his definition does not suggest that art has any relation to beauty and to truth. According to the philosophy that Read is citing, art is "a means" to a specific end: "conceiving the world *visiually*." According to this definition, which probably fits Serge's white painting in the play *Art*, the work of art has forfeited its birthright as disclosing truth and revealing beauty. It has received, in return, acceptance as a means, much as a piece of equipment is a means.

As a means, however, art cannot enhance human existence in the manner that truth and beauty can enhance our daily lives. By holding that art is merely a means, we repeat, Read has forced art to forfeit its birthright. In his trading-off beauty and truth for "conceiving the world *visually*," and in his ardent embracing of a shallow philosophy that justifies works of art that disclose no relation to beauty and truth, Read must accept and justify fake art. What a meager pot of lentil soup!

Need we add that Read's definition, and his discussion that follows the definition, do not relate to the ontological fact that human beings long for beauty and for truth?

Read's definition is dangerous for a worthy existence. Look at it again. You immediately discern that it is a levelling down of art to being a "means of conceiving the world." According to this definition, a work of art has no relation to the spiritual challenges or to the quest for truth or search for beauty which we, as persons, may face. Read does not mention that, for centuries, many of the challenges facing the artist in creating his or her work of art had no relation to the definition that he proffers. During those centuries the challenges facing the artist were firmly linked to the human quest for beauty, for truth, and for spirituality. He ignores the fact that during these centuries works of art often related to the spiritual challenges to which persons may be called to respond. Nor does Read ever suggest that the many ways that great artists responded to these challenges, and found ways to express beauty and truth in their works of art, have added much glory and spirituality to human history.

Consequently, Read's definition of art is sophistry. We should add that this shallow definition allows him, and his many adherents and followers, to evade coping with, and thinking about, the essence of art. This process of evasion is in bad faith. In addition, the arguments of Read and his admirers are sophistry. These sophists attribute to something that is not art, say, Andre's red cedar modules and brick walls, or Jackson Pollock's drip-paintings, the being of art.

Given this sad state of affairs, we again emphasize that we fully agree with those many seminal thinkers, from Parmenides through Socrates to Hegel and Heidegger, who firmly hold that one of the most blessed and worthy ontological distinctions of human beings is that persons long for truth and for beauty. For many, if not most persons, this blessed longing leads to attempts, in their daily lives, to discover, struggle for, unconceal, and express truth, and to create, express, and behold beauty.

These many seminal thinkers also held, often implicitly, that one origin of genuine art is that it is an expression of and a response to the human longing for truth and for beauty. They recognized and stated that when a great work of art, say a beautiful painting by Sandro Botticelli, expresses beauty and truth, it responds to this human longing for truth and for beauty. We agree.

We also agree with the statement, that many of these thinkers added, that a beautiful work of art, which unconceals and expresses truth, adds much glory to human existence and to our history.

Three

HEIDEGGER ON ART, TRUTH, AND BEAUTY

Let us return to the question that emerged at the end of Chapter One: How does the disclosing of truth come about in the work of art — given the tension between the opening up of a world and the elements of Earth? We have given two brief examples of the disclosing of truth in Chapter One, when we discussed the music of George Gershwin and the drama of Tennessee Williams. Still, we agree that this question, concerning the disclosing of truth in a work of genuine art, is one of the most difficult philosophical and practical questions that Heidegger addresses in his essay.

In order to cope with the essence of this difficulty, Heidegger provides a few valuable insights and suggestions concerning the links between truth and its manners of being disclosed to human beings. However, the reader of Heidegger's writings soon realizes that an element of mystery always will remain surrounding the human endeavors which lead to the unconcealment of truth. Probably because of the difficulty of this problem, he addresses the question of truth in many other essays and books. In this book, we only present Heidegger's major insights concerning the unconcealing of truth that appear in "The Origin of the Work of Art."

Heidegger repeatedly points out that the unconcealing of truth is always embedded and rooted in a realm of Being which still remains concealed. Thus, truth always becomes unconcealed in a realm which he calls untruth, a concept which we clarify later in this chapter. Consequently, the world is much broader and more complex and confusing than that specific clearing which is opened, and in which truth is brought forth, say, in a great work of art.

> Rather, the world is the clearing of the paths of the essential guiding directions with which all decision complies. Every decision, however, bases itself on something not mastered, something concealed, confusing; else it would never be a decision.[1]

Consider Michelangelo's well-known sculpture of the Biblical David, which stands in Florence, Italy. The viewer of David encounters a beautiful white marble sculpture of a nude handsome young man, who seems unblemished by age or by struggles in the world. The sensitive viewer also discerns an aura of youthful innocence which shines forth from the white marble sculpture of David. This aura of youthful innocence contributes much to the beauty of Michelangelo's work of art.

Learning from Heidegger, we can state that Michelangelo's sculpture of David establishes a clearing in which the paths of guiding directions, some of them stemming from youthful innocence, can be vividly encountered. These paths can guide a person's decisions, even after youth has passed. But every personal decision, which is guided by youthful innocence, comes into being along the path of life that the person has chosen. Along this path, such a decision frequently bases itself on many not mastered components of each specific person's being and of the situation in which a person finds oneself. These not mastered components of a person's being and situation are frequently concealed, and perhaps even confusing.

Levin, a major figure in Tolstoy's novel *Anna Karenina*, is an example of a young person whose paths of guiding directions frequently stem from youthful innocence. But Tolstoy also shows that all of Levin's personal decisions, which are often guided by youthful innocence that may seem naive, are based on many not mastered aspects of his being and of the situation in which Levin finds himself. This manner of being thrown into the world, to borrow a phrase from Heidegger, in which he was not master of the situation in which he found himself, frequently confused Levin. We believe that it confuses many persons. A similar path of guiding decisions, which are frequently linked to youthful innocence, can be attributed to Alyosha Karamazov, a major character in Dostoyevski's novel, *The Brothers Karamazov.*

An additional example is the youth, David, as he is described in the Bible, who decides to go out and fight Goliath, the giant Philistine warrior. That is the David whom Michelangelo's sculpture has portrayed. The Bible describes David's youthful innocence as bordering on the naive. For instance, David's youthful innocence and naiveness emerges in his discarding the heavy armor with which King Saul attempted to clad him, armor which would, supposedly, guard his body in his upcoming battle with Goliath. David peeled off the armor, which greatly hindered his ability to proceed agilely; he approached Goliath armed only with his staff, his sling, and five smooth stones.

The careful reader of the Biblical story, that is related in First Samuel, immediately discerns that much is concealed in the situation described. Why did David, seemingly at the spur of a moment, decide to fight Goliath for all Israel? Why did King Saul allow him, an unexperienced unarmed youth, a shepherd with no experience of armed conflict, to represent the army of Israel against the giant armor-clad Philistine warrior, Goliath? There are no answers to these questions in the Bible. The story also indicates that before the battle, David's possibility of a surprising victory was concealed from King Saul and from all of Israel, including David's brothers, including David himself.

Michelangelo's sculpture is of the nude youthful David holding his sling. The sculpture unconceals truths about all youthful innocence, and about the world that courageous innocent youths may face. Like David, many of today's youths believe, and many youths have always believed, that their throbbing vital strengths and their limited inhibitions and experience, together with a technical knack in using various simple arms, such as a sling, can bring them victory and glory. This simple truth, which is unconcealed in the clearing opened up by Michelangelo's sculpture of David, contributes much to the beauty of the sculpture. The truth is grasped intuitively; it shines forth from the sculpture of David that Michelangelo formed in white marble.

Thus, we can partially answer the above question. The disclosing of truth comes about in each great work of art through its being able to appeal to and relate to each person's longing for specific truths that are meaningful to his or her Being-in-the-world. What emerges from the above statement is not a vicious circle, but rather a linking of great art to the search for truth, knowledge, and wisdom, a linking already recognized by Plato. A person who longs for truth, who views the encompassing beings that he or she encounter with wonder, and who wonders as to the Being of these beings — such a person may often seek for the truths that great works of art can disclose. Learning from Heidegger, in these two chapters, we have suggested a few of the specific truths that emerge when viewing Michelangelo's sculpture of David, Van Gogh's painting of a peasant woman's pair of shoes, George Gershwin's music, Tennessee Williams's drama, and other great works of art.

Heidegger is correct in indicating that, when a person attempts to find the truth that may be unconcealed in a work of art, this attempt is linked to a personal decision concerning his or her existence. Furthermore, he is correct to hold that, like all seeking for wisdom, the search for unconcealed truth takes place within a realm of untruth. Still, when the truth shines forth, say, from the white marble of Michelangelo's statue of David, or from Edward Hopper's painting, "Nighthawks," the searcher for unconcealed truth will often be dazzled by the beauty of the work of art.

We have been dazzled by the beauty and the youthful innocence shining forth from Michelangelo's David. We have been dazzled by the truths about human alienation shining forth from Edward Hopper's "Nighthawks." Need we add, that no such gleaming and illuminating beauty, and no such disclosing of a truth that relates to paths of guiding directions which persons may encounter, emerges from the works of fake art that we have repeatedly rejected and admonished?

We do want to state categorically that the examples we have given of sophistry in twentieth-century art, say, Carl Andre's brick walls and tin and red cedar modules, Andy Warhol's painting of a can of Campbell's Soup, and Jasper Johns's paintings of American flags, of maps, and of targets — these examples are not only fake art. These works of sophistry themselves reside in the realm of untruth.

Our partial answer to the above question concerning the disclosing of truth brings us very close to the thinking of Plato, especially to the allegory of the cave that is described in the seventh book of *The Republic*. In that allegory, a person who abandons the realm of shadows to which he or she was chained, and emerges from the cave, encounters the blinding illumination of the Good, an illumination which includes recognition of and the seeing of beauty and truth. A great work of art, as mentioned, can also dazzle us with its beauty and truth. Can anyone say, in good faith, that the tin or red cedar modules of Andre, or the paintings of Campbell's Soup by Warhol, or the flags, maps, and targets of Johns, or the drip-paintings by Pollock, or the abstract design-paintings of Miro, or any other of the many works of sophistry in twentieth-century art, have dazzled him or her with their beauty and unconcealed truth? We doubt it!

Heidegger clarifies that, in relation to truth, "Concealment can be a refusal or merely a dissembling."[2] Thus, the person who wishes to unconceal truth, or to bring forth truth from concealment must struggle against both the refusal of truth to become unconcealed and the dissembling of truth in nature and in society. How is truth dissembled in society and in art?

According to the Random House Dictionary, to dissemble is "to give a false appearance to; conceal the real nature of." Look now at Plato's final definition of the sophist in his dialogue, *Sophist*, which is dedicated to clarifying and defining both sophistry and the personality and vocation of the sophist. That definition states that the sophist is a dissembler of the art of self-contradiction.

Earlier in the dialogue, Plato suggests that when a person faces a genuine moment of self-contradiction, the moment can be the first step to educating that person to think, to seek for the truth, and, perhaps, to attain knowledge and wisdom. Here Plato reveals one reason why Socrates was a great educator; because he led people to face genuine moments of self-contradiction, which could have led to the disclosing of truth and to knowledge. As Plato shows in *Theaetetus*, such self-contradiction can also lead to the modest wisdom in which you know that you do not know. In contrast to Socrates, the sophist's dissembling art of self-contradiction does not lead to truth, to thinking, or to wisdom. The sophist, Plato explains, dissembles the genuine self-contradiction, and uses this dissembled self-contradiction to gain his political ends. (All the sophists that Plato described were men.) For instance, the sophist teaches future political leaders methods of leading an adversary to self-contradiction, methods that may help a politician obtain a rhetorical victory.

By such a dissembling of the genuine self-contradiction, the sophist conceals the educational value of self-contradiction, and ignores its significance for the pursuit of wisdom. Consequently, Plato holds, sophistry is a mere imitation of appearance, in this case it is an immitation of self-contradiction. Hence, he adds, sophistry is the art of juggling words. Put succinctly, in human society, truth is dissembled by those who choose to be sophists, who choose to juggle words and merely imitate what appears. We can declare categorically: The sophist is not concerned with unconcealing truth or with thinking.

We have repeatedly stated that the works of many famous twentieth-century painters, such as Jasper Johns, Andy Warhol, Roy Lichtenstein, Piet Mondrian, Jackson Pollock, Joan Miro, Ben Nicholson, are sophistry. Their sophistry consists in the fact that these painters are dissemblers of the Being of true art. By their dissembling, they give a false appearance to art. The Being of genuine art, according to Heidegger, includes an unconcealing of truth. However, these painters produce works which testify that their producers do not relate to the Being of genuine art. We repeat: they are dissemblers of art. The works of these sophists consist of a juggling of colors and forms. Not one of the works of these sophists in the realm of art, sophists who call themselves artists, unconceals a worthy truth. Nor are their works beautiful.

We have reached a crucial impasse. The works of those contemporary painters and sculptors which we attack, are in direct conflict with Heidegger's thinking on what is the essence and the origin of the work of art. Borrowing a locution from Plato, we can state that these painters and sculptors are primarily artists of sophistry whose main goal is producing works that are based on the dissembling art. Their works are fakes because, instead of unconcealing truths, they conceal truths.

What truths do the works of fake art conceal?

Among the truths concealed by fake art is the major truth about the essence of a work of art that Heidegger has formulated: A great work of art unconceals truth and is beautiful. Heidegger also points out: "The establishing of truth in the work is the bringing forth of a being such as never was before and will never be again."[3] Cézanne painted the portrait of his wife a few times; he painted apples and other simple objects many times. The greatness of each of these paintings is that each one, be it of his wife or of apples, brings "forth a being such as never was before and will never be again." That bringing forth of the truth of a being is one of the secrets of Cézanne's excellence as an artist.

All the works of sophistry produced by the dissemblers of art in the twentieth century, including those we have attacked, conceal this major truth, that the genuine work of art unconceals truth and is beautiful. In the writings of the sophists who support these works, we have uncovered a tendency to indoctrinate the reader to accept false ideas. They ignore the fact that, in the process of presenting paintings and sculptures that dissemble art, the twentieth-century producers of works of fake art repeatedly conceal the nature and the essence of painting and of sculpture, as an art that unconceals truth, illuminates truth, and presents beauty. Moreover, these so-called artists know that you cannot relate the above citation from Heidegger to their works, be they cans of Campbell's Soup or abstract patterns by Mondrian and Ben Nicholson. None of the works produced by these sophists brings "forth a being such as never was before and never will be again."

Why was Plato angry at the sophists, some of whom appeared periodically in Athens from other Greek cities, and enticed the youth to learn and to practice rhetoric? Because they distorted truths and disparaged the search for truth, for knowledge, and for wisdom. Why are we angry at the sophistry in the works of so-called art produced by many of the twentieth-century painters and sculptors — Warhol, Pollock, Andre, Lichtenstein, Johns, Miro, Mondrian, and many others — whose uninspiring works clutter museums and galleries? Because these sophists produce, present, and display works that distort the essence of art, which should unconceal truth and present beauty.

Thus, the sophistry that prevails in thousands of works that are called twentieth-century art is destructive of many things that enhance and glorify human existence, among them wisdom, beauty, and truth. According to Heidegger, the struggle to open up a clearing in which truth will become unconcealed is the primal conflict that we human beings face. This primal conflict, this struggle for truth, this ontological spiritual challenge does not concern the sophists who thrive in every generation, be they those professional sophists whom Plato and Socrates repeatedly attacked, or the contemporary painters and sculptors whose works we reject and condemn in this book. Once again we wish to state that, like the ancient seducing sophists, whom Plato seems to have despised, those twentieth-century producers of works of fake art are sophists who bring forth works that are not an unconcealment of truth. Hence, these works of sophistry are a rejection of those things that are worthy in themselves, such as truth, wisdom, and beauty.

This finding is central to our attack on sophistry in twentieth-century art. It reveals that no primal conflict for opening up a clearing where truth may be unconcealed is found in the so-called works of art produced by the painters and sculptors whom we are attacking and condemning as sophists and dissemblers. Hence, we can state categorically that the works of those applauded twentieth-century painters and sculptors, such as Johns, Pollock, Mondrian, Lichtenstein, Miro, Andre, and Stella are sophistry. They are not genuine art, because the works are both a refusal of truth and a dissembling of truth. These fake works of art also disregard beauty. It is not surprising, therefore, that the painters of these works often relate contemptuously to beauty.

We have stumbled upon another seemingly simple and partial answer to the above question concerning the disclosing of truth in a work of art. In order for this disclosing of truth to come about, the artist must struggle not to succumb to the lures of sophism. Furthermore, in creating works of art, artists must personally participate in the primal conflict that opens up a clearing in which truth can be unconcealed in the work that they are creating. Put differently, artists must comprehend that their vocation, their calling, requires a daily struggle. In their life and in their attempts to create a work of art, they must struggle to unconceal truth, and to express this truth in a beautiful work of art. We can add that the disclosing of truth in a work of art, with the tensions that are involved in this disclosing, at times, may reflect the tension in the life of the artist who struggles to unconceal truths.

Yet, we want to repeat a former statement. Despite the many worthy insights that Heidegger has presented on the links between truth and art, it is still evident that the ability of human beings to unconceal truth, by creating a genuine and beautiful work of art, remains much of a mystery. In this book, we acknowledge this mystery, while catching glimpses of some of its significant components.

How is beauty linked to truth? That also is much of a mystery. We can say that Heidegger's discussion of truth in "The Origin of the Work of Art" relates to the beauty of the work and its linkage to truth. He states: "*Beauty is one way in which truth occurs as unconcealedness.*"[4]

Heidegger explains that the work of art is one way by which human beings make the unconcealedness of truth happen, by opening a clearing in which a specific truth can be seen. Van Gogh's painting of a peasant woman's shoes reveals truths about equipment, and about the peasant woman's daily life; Michelangelo's statue of David reveals truths about youthful innocence, and its link to courageous deeds of some youths. Hopper's haunting painting, "Nighthawks," and many of his other beautiful paintings, disclose truths about the loneliness and aloneness of many persons in our alienated contemporary life. We would add that the beauty of a great work of art is firmly linked to such revelations of truths, and that these revelations are one of the ways by which truths may become unconcealed. As Heidegger suggests, we also believe that some truths can only be unconcealed in a great work of art. This unique revelation of truth is crucial for beauty to emerge in a work of art. Thus, the human striving to unconceal truth, and especially truth about human existence, is one of the origins of the work of art.

For a negative example that supports Heidegger's ideas, consider again the famous Giza pyramids and the Sphinx, that stand on the outskirts of Cairo in Egypt. These architectural monstrosities may astonish their viewers, but they unconceal no truth to today's observer. The Giza pyramids and the Sphinx are indifferent to truth; hence they convey nothing to their many observers. Furthermore, the works of Egyptologists and of historians of ancient Egyptian art that we have consulted never mention the pyramids and the Sphinx as disclosing a truth. Because no truth shines forth from the pyramids, or from the Sphinx, they are not beautiful. Hence, we can strengthen the point made in Chapter One, and again state that the Giza pyramids and the Sphinx are assuredly not works of art.

We are now able better to understand the ontology of the creative act that brings forth a work of genuine art. Recall that the beauty of a work of art is partially an expression of the happening of truth in that work. This happening of truth is necessary. Without it the work is not beautiful, and we hold that it is not a work of art. On the basis of this description of the work of art, Heidegger points out that the nature of creating a work of art must be linked to the nature of truth as the unconcealing of beings, and also as partially disclosing the Being of beings. The genuine artist has a passion for unconcealing truth and expresses this passion in his or her work. This determination concerning the creation of a work of art clearly distinguishes the creating of a work of art from the making of a piece of equipment. When you make a piece of equipment, say, a hammer, or a pencil, or a rocket, no truth, as the unconcealedness of beings, emerges.

Yet, Heidegger is still unsatisfied with his generalization that links the work of art to truth as the unconcealedness of beings. He decides to look more carefully at the nature of truth and at its link to the creation of a work of art. He asks: "how does the impulse toward such a thing as a work [of art] lie in the nature of truth? Of what nature is truth, that it can be set into work, or even under certain conditions must be set into work, in order to be *as* truth?" [5] In order to partially respond to these questions, he again turns to discuss truth and its links to untruth.

Heidegger recognizes that these questions require examining the process of creation which brings forth the work of art. How does this process of creation differ from the process which brings forth a piece of equipment? After all, as Heidegger acknowledges, skills and good craftmanship are crucial both for creating a great work of art and for bringing forth a new usable piece of equipment. The superb shoemaker is a good craftsman with leather, hammer and awl, much as the great painter, say, Jean Chardin, had superb skills with pencils, brushes, and paints. Despite the famous rebellion of Marcel Duchamp and others, a rebellion which led to the fact that pieces of equipment, like Duchamp's urinal, currently hang and stand in many museums and are called art — despite this widespread inanity, we firmly hold, together with Heidegger, that Chardin's paintings differ, in their essence, from a good pair of shoes.

What constitutes this difference? The question leads us back to Heidegger's description of the work of art, which prompts us to answer: In Chardin's paintings a beauty can be discerned, because in these paintings truth occurs as unconcealedness, and truths are disclosed about the Being of specific beings. No such beauty in which truth occurs as unconcealedness is found in the good pair of shoes, made by the shoemaker.

The craftmanship in the piece of equipment is tested by the usability, of that piece of equipment for specific human beings. If the shoes do not fit, if they do not last long, the shoemaker is not good at making shoes. If astronomers discover that the Hubble telescope does not function well, the people who built the telescope are in trouble. The superb skills of Hopper or of Vermeer, to which their paintings testify, have no link to utility. The painter's painting skills are revealed when the beauty of the painting, say in Hopper's "Nighthawks" or in Vermeer's "View of Delft," is evident. At times, this beauty will dazzle the viewer. This beauty includes truth as unconcealedness about the Being of the beings that have been painted.

Heidegger enlarges upon this idea by introducing a new concept, which is linked to much that he has discussed: the Open. In the great painting, he suggests, the painter's skill will establish what he calls the Open. In contrast, when creating a piece of equipment, good craftsmanship never establishes the Open.

What is the Open? According to Heidegger, when the struggle for truth as unconcealment is won, the Open appears as a realm in which that truth shows itself. In the genuine work of art, say a painting, the Open is that limited space found in the painting in which truth is unconcealed. In that space, in the Open, the tension between the opened world and the elements of Earth bring about the unconcealing of truth about the Being of certain specific beings. In "Nighthawks," and in other paintings by Hopper, truths about the loneliness and aloneness of persons in contemporary life are unconcealed. Each painting serves as the Open for these truths to show themselves.

To better clarify the Open, Heidegger returns to the link between truth and untruth. He adds that the Open, and the truth about a being which is disclosed in the Open, emerges in the broad realm of untruth that encompasses that specific truth. Note that the term "untruth," as Heidegger uses it in his writings, does not mean deceit or lies. By the untruth, he means the realm of what he denotes as the not-yet-uncovered, or the un-uncovered. Thus, for many centuries, during which astronomers gazed at the heavens and studied the movements of the stars and the planets, Kepler's laws on planetary movement were situated in the realm of the untruth. They emerged from this realm after Kepler discovered them and formulated them. The painter or the sculptor who is skilled in his or her vocation, for instance, Michelangelo, will often win the struggle to bring forth truth from untruth in his or her work. The great sculptor or painter is victorious in this struggle. By this victory, the painter or sculptor will establish the Open in the work of art. Thus, the nature of truth is such that it is disclosed only in the Open, and a great work of art, say, Michelangello's David or his painting of the ceiling of the Sistine Chapel, establishes the Open.

In contrast, in a work of fake art there is no struggle to bring forth truth from untruth. As we have already shown, and as many of the producers of the works of twentieth-century art that we reject frequently admit, the work that they produce is often a gimmick, a trick, a presentation of something weird, popular, mind-boggling, astonishing. What struggle to bring forth truth from untruth, or to establish the Open, can be discerned in any Minimalist painting, including the totally white painting that Serge purchased in the play *Art*?

As a term, "the Open" should not surprise us. Probably, we have all experienced the many difficulties of opening a fellow person to certain truths that have become evident to us, or, in Heidegger's terms, have become unconcealed. Many of Plato's Socratic dialogues show Socrates facing disturbing and, at times, dangerous and frustrating difficulties in his attempts to open fellow Athenians to truths that he endeavored to bring forth from concealment. Still, a few of the Platonic dialogues, say, *The Republic* and *Phaedrus*, are optimistic. They reveal that, at times, a new realm of openness emerges between the participants in the dialogue when the truths that Socrates is presenting become unconcealed, and the participants accept these truths. With Heidegger we can say that, through dialogue, Socrates strove to establish the Open in which he disclosed truths, but this Open was always encompassed by a realm of untruth, a realm in which Socrates admitted that he did not know the truths. Only in the Open that he succeeded in establishing Socrates showed his partners in dialogue truths that had become unconcealed.

Can we not say, therefore, that a great painting or sculpture can also establish a sort of dialogue with its viewers in which the Open emerges and truths slowly become unconcealed? That possible interpretation could perhaps emerge from Heidegger's writings. We should add that this interpretation of Heidegger's term, the Open, suggests a closeness to the views of Martin Buber, which we do not discuss.[6]

Here, however, we want to stress Heidegger's belief that central to the great painter's creativity is the unconcealing of truth and the establishment of the Open in which that truth is unconcealed. The viewer of, say, the paintings of Balthus, Van Gogh, and Chardin relates to the Open that he or she encounters in a specific painting, and will find in it truth that is unconcealed. Heidegger would probably hold that the great painter's creativity and skills are directed primarily towards the possibility of unconcealing truth and establishing the Open in the specific painting that he or she is currently painting.

The sensitive viewer will quite rapidly discern that much of the twentieth-century art that we are attacking is hardly based on superb skills in painting or sculpting. Nor do these works of fake art make any attempts to establish the Open. Consequently, we do not apprehend much of what Heidegger would call the truths that can be unconcealed by creativity and by superb artistic skills in many contemporary so-called works of art. Is it a wonder that we condemn these works as sophistry?

Consider, for instance, Frank Stella's work, "New Madrid," painted in 1961. On a plain bright red square background, Stella painted a white line that starts at the top right edge of the red square and creates seemingly concentric white squares that become smaller and smaller until, close to the center, the white line stops. Conversely, you could say that the white line starts from the center and by creating concentric squares continues to the top edge of the red square. Why Stella named this work "New Madrid" is not clear. Whatever one thinks of this painting, it is evident that there is no need for superb painting skills here. Nor can you discern any Open in which truth becomes unconcealed in "New Madrid."

In contrast to Stella's work that does not require skills, an anecdote relates that it took the young, twelve-year old Michelangelo six years of daily practice to become acquainted with what can be achieved when working with a chisel in marble. Nothing of such a skill was needed in order to paint Stella's "New Madrid."

Indeed, in his many works, Stella never reaches a level of artistic skill that even partially resembles the skill that was needed to paint, say, Edward Hopper's or Balthus's paintings. Nor does the term creative, as Heidegger defined it, relate to "New Madrid." Because, as mentioned, in Stella's so-called work of art, you will not comprehend the Open, in which truths about beings becomes unconcealed. Nor does "New Madrid" reveal the tension between Earth and the opening up of a world that is needed for truth to be unconcealed and for beauty to be evident in a work of art. At best, "New Madrid" is an interesting gimmick, a playing with illusions, or with delusions. It is a fake work of art that has been painted with the equipment that a genuine artist uses.

Someone may ponder our conclusions and ask: Are you suggesting that many of those twentieth-century painters and sculptors, whom you are attacking and calling sophists, are poor craftsmen? Do you believe that one of the reasons these painters and sculptors produced what you call works of sophistry in twentieth-century art is that they lacked the skills to create great art? Our answer to both questions is: Yes. We truly believe that, in addition to other failings, probably most of the producers of sophistry in the realm of art during the twentieth century lacked the talents, the skills, and the perseverence that are required to create great art.

Thus, we hold that many of the twentieth-century painters and sculptors whom we term sophists are not gifted with the skills and talents necessary to be great painters and sculptors. Consequently, they do not have the skills which are needed to unconceal truth, to establish the Open in their works, and to create a work of beauty. It does not help them that they rely on tricks, play with illusions, present gimmicks, and rely on sophistry to present their uninspiring, vacuous, and often banal productions. The results of their sophistry are productions that are inferior to works of genuine great art, say by Picasso or by Rembrandt.

We will not continue to present Heidegger's discussion concerning the work of art. His major thoughts and ideas that are relevant to the essence of the work of art, and that partially reveal the current widespread sophistry in art, which ignores this essence, have been presented. His ideas on the tension between Earth and world that helps unconceal truth have shown us the inferior status of works like those of Carl Andre, Frank Stella, Minimalist artists, and many others.

On the basis of Heidegger's illuminating ideas, we have firmly rejected the many works of sophistry that abound in contemporary art galleries and museums. We have indicated that these works do not unconceal truth, are not beautiful, and hence, are devoid of spirituality. The tension between Earth and the opening up of a world does not emerge in these banal and uninspiring works. We are quite sure, however, that our rejection of sophistry in twentieth-century art can be broadened and deepened in ways that will complement and support Heidegger's important thoughts and insights. The source of our belief is our recognizing that there is more to say about the widespread sophistry that we encounter when viewing many works of twentieth-century art found in museums and galleries.

As a result of what we have learned from Heidegger's essay, and based on what we learned from Plato about sophistry, we would suggest that not only the works of sophistry in twentieth-century art must be rejected and condemned as fakes. As mentioned, in his dialogue *Sophist*, Plato defines the sophist and firmly repudiates and disparages him as a person, together with the sophistry that he authors and endeavors to spread. Plato convinced us that we must not only attack the works of fake art. We must also cut off all relations with sophists, condemn them, and daily fight against their deceit, since they destroy what is worthy for human existence.

In order to better comprehend the destructiveness of sophistry in twentieth-century art, we turn to a short chapter on the curse of indifference — a curse that emanates from many works of sophistry in twentieth-century art. That chapter will help us to see how the works of sophistry that spread and encourage indifference are ruinous of personality. The link between art and personality will be presented in later chapters, when we turn to the thinking of Nicolas Berdyaev.

Four

SOPHISTRY IN ART AND INDIFFERENCE

> The Church condemns violence, but it condemns
> indifference more harshly. Violence can be the
> expression of love, indifference never. One is an
> imperfection of charity the other the perfection of
> egoism.[1]
>
> Graham Greene, *The Comedians*

The works of twentieth-century art that we are attacking are indifferent to the human pursuit of excellence, which includes the ongoing quest – that some people in each generation undertake — for justice, love, beauty, wisdom, knowledge, freedom, and truth. Consequently, these works of fake art are also indifferent to history, and to much evil that is currently occurring in the world. Some of these works of sophistry are so indifferent to the Being of the beings in our world that they border on the autistic. One immediate result is that the works of fake art impoverish the museums and galleries, because the area in the museum and gallery in which they are on display emanates a basic irresponsibility for the world, in addition to being devoid of beauty, truth, and spirituality.

Look again at a few of those works of fake art that we have repeatedly disparaged, rejected, and condemned — Roy Lichtenstein's enlarged comics, Andy Warhol's paintings of a can of Campbell's Soup, Jasper Johns's paintings of an American flag or map and of targets, Piet Mondrian's paintings of abstract color patterns, Frank Stella's painting, "New Madrid," described in the Chapter Three, Jackson Pollock's large canvasses of drip-paintings, the large banal installations that often take up entire rooms in a museum, the vacuous and ugly so-called sculptures that stand outside many corporate headquarters — these and many other works of sophistry can be recognized by their inherent and boldly expressed indifference to history and to the human quest for excellence.

To give just one example of the indifference of fake art, Piet Mondrian painted many of his abstract paintings which feature colored lines and patterns during, and after the terrifying experience of World War I. He also painted his abstract works in the years that Nazism was on the rise in Germany, and fascism was triumphant in Italy and Spain. He continued to paint these abstract patterns of colors in the years that Nazism and fascism had conquered large areas of Europe, oppressing and murdering millions of people, establishing concentration camps and death camps, implementing genocide, and performing many other crimes, horrors, and unprecedented evils. Nothing of this terrible history emerges in Mondrian's paintings. Hence, his works are not only spiritually vacuous; they are also totally indifferent to the crimes, evils, and horrors that occurred while Mondrian was painting.

In stark contrast to the works produced by Mondrian, during the same four decades of the twentieth century that commenced with World War I, Max Beckman and Otto Dix, each in his own style, were also creating paintings and other works of visual art. Their paintings include a forceful response to the terrible evils that they witnessed and firmly condemned. Let us say it again. The haunting beauty of many of the works by Beckman and Dix include personal responses to the truths that had become unconcealed by the pernicious historical developments that these sensitive artists repeatedly witnessed. Put succinctly, their works of art frequently express a deep concern about the crimes, the evils, and the horror which Beckman and Dix encountered in the encompassing world, a world in which the many evils arising from greed, jingoism, fascism, racism, totalitarianism, and Nazism often reigned unchallenged.

Consequently, all of Mondrian's abstract paintings are vacuous, historically irrelevant, and totally indifferent to the world in which they were painted. Yet, those abstract paintings were the only works that he painted. The truth about Mondrian, the so-called famous painter of abstract paintings, is sad and revealing. For four decades he painted dozens of paintings that are not beautiful and are totally indifferent to truths about the terrible historical events which characterized his European society during those decades. — Precisely these truths quite often scream out from the beautiful works of art created by Beckman and Dix. We return to Mondrian's indifference in Chapter Nine.

Someone may ask: How does indifference emanate from the Being of the work of which you call fake art? How does this indifference influence the viewers of these works?

Learning from Heidegger, we have already shown that these works of fake art are indifferent to the origin of the work of art, to the tension between the opening up of a world and the elements of Earth, and, especially, to the fact that a work of art should be beautiful and should unconceal truth. We also clarified that beauty and the unconcealing of truth constitute a major origin of a work of great art, and do not exist in the works of fake art. However, we did not mention that the indifference conveyed by many of the works of sophistry in twentieth-century art includes an indifference to the person viewing the work of art. This indifference is ontological. It stems from the works of fake art being indifferent to the fact that every one of their viewers is endowed with freedom and with the possibility of striving to be a person who is a spiritual being. We have already indicated that when we say "a person who is a spiritual being" we mean a person who longs for and seeks to realize and relate to beauty and to truth. Such a person may also relate to and attempt to realize justice, love, knowledge, freedom, wisdom, and other things that are worthy in themselves. In many instances, therefore, the pursuit of excellence is linked to spiritual existence.

Our personal experience, that we have obtained while conducting research for this book, has revealed that it is not difficult to comprehend the aura of indifference that emanates from many works of fake art. Just look at them. You will immediately perceive that these works of fake art hardly ever invite the observer to share beauty; nor do they appeal to the person looking at them to relate to certain truths; nor do they relate to other things that are worthy in themselves; nor do they establish the Open or open up a world for their observers. The works of sophistry hang there or stand there in a gallery or a museum and convey their indifference to beauty and to truth to their observers. Many observers sense this indifference and, at times, they absorb it. To further comprehend this indifference, all you need to do is to visit a museum where twentieth-century works of sophistry are on display, beside, say, works of genuine art such as paintings by Tintoretto, Canaletto, Guardi, or Matisse.

At that museum, take a few moments and pay attention to those persons who are passing through the galleries in which those works of sophistry in twentieth-century art are displayed. You will quite rapidly discover that almost all the persons pass by these works of sophistry quite nonchalantly, unconcernedly, without stopping to look carefully, without being authentically engrossed. What can you discover when you look carefully at a Minimalist painting, or at one of Joan Miro's abstract designs, or at one of Warhol's paintings of a can of Campbell's Soup? Nothing!

Many of the observers of these works seem disinterested, as if what is exhibited in the gallery, at most, may arouse inquisitiveness. Borrowing a term from Heidegger, you can say that these observers float past works of fake art, without becoming engaged, much as a stick floats disengagedly downstream, past a cliff, a clump of water lilies, a bridge. The reason for such floating is quite evident. When encountering a work of sophistry, the person observing the work intuitively perceives, that there is not even a spark of hope, that the work may appeal to his or her quest for spirituality. Put differently, the person in the gallery never senses that one personally may be inspired by these works to strive to enhance one's existence. Instead, the person viewing works of fake art grasps that these so-called artistic pieces are merely a thing, or perhaps a clever ploy, or a smart hoax, exhibited so as to arouse his or her curiosity, or to serve as an ambiguous topic for idle talk. Here is an example of a clever ploy that was exhibited in a London art gallery.

An essay in *The Economist* of 9 June 2001, describes and discusses the so-called art of Cornelia Parker, who specializes in producing and exhibiting wierd installations. Here is a paragraph from the essay.

> Ms Parker shot to attention in 1995 with "The Maybe", a coffin like glass case at London's Serpentine gallery in which an actress, Tilda Swinton, slept during the day, lying in state like a living relic. "The idea of sleeping

> evoked the idea of life and death, that we're always in
> this limbo," explains Ms Parker. Ms Swinton was
> surrounded with relics of famous dead people who had
> become icons in an earlier age, including Freud, Queen
> Victoria, and Charles Dickens.

It is not difficult to see that Cornelia Parker's "The Maybe" is a no more than a clever ploy, which arouses curiosity and idle talk. It also is evident that "The Maybe" is not beautiful, does not unconceal truth, and does not establish the Open that Heidegger discusses. Parker never suggested that such may have been her intentions or achievement. Nor has this installation, despite Parker's shallow attempt to provide an explanation, any relationship to spirituality.

Unfortunately, wierd and cunning installations are common. Like "The Maybe," these contemporary works of fake art may be clever ploys. But they are remote, bleak, and spiritually uninspiring; as such, they frequently convey indifference. Indeed, if you stand and look at "The Maybe," what truths will you discover? None.

In contrast, many a person may stand quite a few moments deeply absorbed in looking at and relating with his or her entire being to one of the beautiful paintings of Tintoretto, Canaletto, Guardi, or Matisse. You can often feel how the beauty and the truth emanating from some of these works of genuine art can elevate and inspire your being. We firmly hold that such great works of art, in a mysterious way, can indicate to you the possibility of living a nobler and more worthy mode of existence.

If you are not yet convinced as to the indifference emanating from the works of sophistry in twentieth-century art that are on display in a museum, take the time to hearken to the phrases that people use to respond to these works. According to our findings, the most favorable responses to such works are words that lack personal commitment, and do not express a person's longing for beauty, for truth, or for other things that are worthy in themselves. Here is a list of the more frequent words that we heard, when listening to observers expressing their personal response in a gallery or a museum, as they stood briefly before a work of fake art: "interesting," "curious," "amazing," "astonishing," "strange," "shocking," "startling," "alluring," "provocative." However, as depicted in Yasmina Reza's play, *Art*, which we briefly described in the Introduction, when listening to persons viewing fake art, quite often you may hear, as we have heard, derogatory words: "shit," "crap," "deceit," "fake," "embarrassing," "meaningless," "worthless." If you listen carefully, you may also discern that even these curses and derogatory locutions are often muttered unconcernedly, without personal commitment. Note that neither the favorable nor the unfavorable responses are in any way similar to the responses that you may hear from a person who is viewing paintings by Tintoretto, Canaletto, Guardi, or Matisse. Here you may hear words like "beautiful," "inspiring," "lovely," "elegant," "profound," "graceful," "worthy," "true," and in the case of paintings by Matisse, "joyful."

Our hearkening to phrases that people use when relating to art is not a mere listening to what Heidegger calls idle talk. Language, after all, helps us to describe and to relate to the Being of beings. Also, language is most significant if we wish to describe and relate to the Being of works of art. When persons spontaneously announce that certain works that are hanging in a museum amaze, or startle, or provoke, when these works are only clever, or curious, or interesting — these words suggest that the works which they describe do not relate to any of the authentic possibilities of Being which may engage the person who encountered them. For instance, the works of Cornelia Parker, or Andy Warhol, or Jasper Johns do not evoke in the viewer a commitment for the search for excellence. Nor do they appeal to his or her longing for beauty and for truth. Nor, as mentioned in our above critique of the works of Mondrian, do these works convey the need and the call, quite often expressed by a genuine artist, to assume responsibility for history and for what is happening in the world. Thus, like Mondrian's painted patterns, Jackson Pollock's dozens of abstract drip-paintings, and many other twentieth-century works of sophistry exude an aura of indifference and irresponsibility for the fate of the world which these so-called artists shared with us.

Contrast these works of sophistry with Picasso's famous painting "Guernica" and with some of the paintings by Edward Hopper that portray the profound alienation and aloneness that are frequently found in much contemporary life. You will immediately perceive that, unlike the indifferent works of fake art painted by Mondrian and Pollock, the paintings of Picasso and Hopper frequently convey a call for responsibility to relate to and to alter the world in which we live, in which so much evil, loneliness, and alienation prevail.

We are not alone in describing certain works of modern art as objects that convey indifference. Consider a literary example from Graham Greene's moving novel, *The Human Factor*, which describes the inner workings of the British Secret Service.

In one scene in the novel, Doctor Percival, a top agent in the British Secret Service and a medical doctor, wants to convince Daintry, the internal security agent of their organization, to be indifferent to a murder that Percival will commit. With the complicity of their commander, Percival intends to insidiously poison a member of the British Secret Service who is supposedly a double agent and is passing on information to the Soviet Union. This planned murder, of a man whom Daintry must identify, will be based on flimsy evidence; it will be performed discreetly. This punishment will be meted out without putting the suspected informer on trial, without giving him a fair chance to prove his innocence, and without full proof that the man is indeed the informer whom they are seeking. The entire situation deeply disturbs Daintry, who believes in honesty, fairness, and the due process of law.

Percival senses Daintry's qualms. He wants to calm him and finds Daintry in a room in which hangs a painting by Ben Nicholson – whose abstract paintings of squares of colors bring to mind the abstract patterns of Mondrian. Percival suggests to Daintry to look carefully at the Nicholson painting and to learn from it to be indifferent to the crime that will be committed:

> "Take a look at that Nicholson. Such a clever balance. Squares of different colour. And yet living happily together. No clash. The man has a wonderful eye. Change just one of the colours – even the size of the square, and it would be no good at all." Percival pointed to a yellow square. "There's your Section 6. That's your square from now on. You don't need to worry about the blue and the red. All you have to do is pinpoint our man and then tell me. You've no responsibility for what happens in the blue or the red squares. In fact not even in the yellow. You just report. No bad conscience. No guilt."[2]

Thus, according to Graham Greene, those works of twentieth-century art that resemble the paintings of Ben Nicholson can teach us to be indifferent to a planned murder!

We can pull together our above observations. The person viewing works of sophistry in twentieth-century art is encouraged by the works that he or she is perceiving to be passive and indifferent. In addition, the observer of works of sophistry in twentieth-century art may often accept as final the ugly and wicked reality which he or she encounters, both in the works of fake art which are exhibited in a gallery or hang in a room, and in the world in which he or she live. Consequently, quite frequently people respond to the indifference emanating from the work of fake art with an uncommitted curiosity, or with passivity and disinteredness. These responses are usually components of personal indifference.

We also have observed that this encouraging of personal indifference by certain works of sophistry in twentieth-century art infects the atmosphere prevailing in the entire gallery in which these works of fake art are on display. Hence, as mentioned, this indifference impoverishes the museum as a meeting place where people can relate to beauty, to truth, and to other things that are worthy in themselves. The infectious atmosphere of indifference in these galleries is another reason that most viewers pass by works of fake art nonchalantly; they float through the gallery without engaging themselves, and without committing themselves to an attempt to relate wholeheartedly to the works that they apprehend.

If we again contrast these attitudes to what happens when a person encounters a beautiful work of art that unconceals truth, say, by Tintoretto, Canaletto, Guardi, or Matisse, the difference is evident. Frequently, such works of genuine art engage the viewer personally; they address him or her as a spiritual being. In addition, these beautiful works of art may inspire a person to actively seek for additional truths and for other works of art that inspire and convey beauty and unconceal truth. Thus, these genuine works of art may enhance a person's Being-in-the-world. Such a personal encounter and engagement with beauty and with truth, coupled with an ardent seeking for beauty and for truth is, at least partially, the undertaking of a search for excellence. It is also an assuming of responsibility for a world in which beauty and truth are respected and sought.

Learning from Graham Greene, and, at least partially, from Karl Marx, we wish to address a major question concerning the commercial success of fake art. The question emerges when we comprehend two seemingly independent trends in the history of the twentieth century: the reign of brutal capitalism (in the second half of the century, the reign of brutal corporate capitalism) and the widespread financial success of works of fake art. Is there a link between these two trends?

We believe a firm link exists. The question, however, should be put more bluntly: Is it strange that, in the twentieth century, philosophers of art, art critics, journalists covering art exhibits, and art historians, together with wealthy buyers of art supported the creation of and extolling of thousands of works of sophistry, works that convey indifference? We would answer: It is not strange at all!

An intuitive explanation of our answer to the question is not difficult. A regime that prides itself on its encouraging rampant greed and the unjust exploitation of human beings, a regime that persistently seeks ways to justify this greed and unjust exploitation, as the capitalist regime does, strives to perfect and to justify egoism. But, as Greene pointed out in the citation that opens this chapter, indifference is a perfection of egoism. At least, indifference is one of the widely accepted ways to perfect egoism. Hence, works of sophistry in art that convey indifference, and infect their observers with indifference, accord quite well with many of the manifestations of twentieth-century capitalism, especially with its encouraging of egoism and greed.

In a word, the history of purchases of works of art in the twentieth century discloses that wealthy capitalist buyers happily support works of art that convey indifference to their observers. Capitalist corporations also happily contribute to art shows in which sophistry in twentieth-century art prevails. Many corporations also purchase sculptures that are works of sophistry to stand at the entrance to their headquarters. This seemingly concealed link between the brutal greed-inspired capitalist regime and the extolling of fake art is a theme in a recent remarkable movie: "Cradle Will Rock."

Furthermore, as Noam Chomsky has repeatedly shown, widespread political indifference in democratic capitalist-oriented countries, and especially in the United States, also accords with the quite frequently expressed wishes of the princes of corporate capitalism. These contemporary Machivellian princes wish to rule the country, and the world, as an oligarchy. The writings of their many sycophants support the widespread political indifference to what is happening in the world.[3] Is it not evident that this political indifference will spread to and attempt to dominate the realm of art?

Finally, in response to the above question, Marx would probably have suggested, with much more than a trace of truth, that the many works of sophistry that are found in art galleries and museums are an apt expression of the egoistic and individualistic values and attitudes that arise from the corporate capitalist relations of production. Developing this major point, however, is beyond the scope of our study. It would probably require writing another book.

We can partially summarize the destructive influence of indifference in the works of twentieth-century fake art with a sentence fro. Nicolas Berdyaev's autobiography. "Reality is, in fact, closed to those who pretend to know in a state of indifference, disinterestedness, and neutrality, for they suppress the evidence of the very reality which they attempt to know."[4]

We believe that Berdyaev's statement is a true description of both groups of sophists whom we are attacking: the pseudo-artists who produce works that are fake art, for instance, Parker, Nicholson, Miro, Warhol, and Johns, and those many writers on art, such as Arthur Danto, Jacques Barzun, and Herbert Read, who enthusiastically applaud the works of fake art. Both groups pretend to know what art is; but the members of both groups exist in a state of indifference, disinterestedness, and neutrality to the widespread sophistry that has emerged in twentieth-century art. In addition, many of the socially accepted writers on art are also indifferent to the evil and deceit that is widespread in the world that we all share. Hence, the members of both groups of sophists close themselves to large sections of reality.

Furthermore, both groups of sophists suppress the evidence of the reality and the origin of art, which Heidegger painstakingly clarified. They reveal a stark ignorance in relation to Heidegger's ideas about art, yet they indicate that they are specialists in the field of art. For instance, their ignorance is revealed in their refusal to perceive and to acknowledge that the reality of art originates in the human longing for beauty and for truth, and that an origin of the work of art is the unconcealing of truth.

We must, therefore, state categorically: Contrary to the distorted thinking and writing of these sophists, who, as so-called artists, philosophers, historians, critics, and journalists, praise many works of fake art from which an aura of indifference emanates, genuine art will never be indifferent. Indeed, genuine great art discourages indifference; it invites the observer of the work of art to live his or her freedom as a responsible person who seeks truth and beauty and wishes to spread beauty and truth in the world.

Need we add that one major way by which genuine art rejects indifference is by being beautiful, and by its unconcealing of truth?

Five

BERDYAEV: ART AND PERSONALITY

Nicolas Alexandrovitch Berdyaev (in some of the translations of his books into English he is called Nikolai Berdyaev) was born in the city of Kiev in Russia, in 1874, and died in Paris in 1948. In 1922, together with a group of Russian intellectuals, he was exiled from the newly established Soviet Union by the Bolshevik regime. He resided for a few years in Berlin before establishing a permanent residence in Paris. During all the years of his exile, he longed for his beloved Russia, and expressed this longing in his writings.

Berdyaev is probably one of the most neglected major thinkers of the twentieth century.[1] We find few essays on his thought in philosophical journals. In the many books that we have read, which were written by art critics who deal with contemporary art, or by historians of contemporary art, or by philosophers who relate to contemporary art, we have found no reference to any of his ideas. Since many of his books present original and valuable insights and engaging ideas, we have been unable to find a discernable reason for his being marginalized, especially in the past few decades. For instance, almost all of Berdyaev's books, that were translated into English in the middle of the twentieth century, are currently out of print.

Berdyaev repeatedly announced that he was primarily a philosopher of religion. He developed a philosophy of history and of eschatology which are slanted toward Christianity, and which present the Christian message, as he understood it. His deep faith in the truths of Christianity and in the message of Jesus informs this philosophy of history and eschatology. But for a contemporary philosopher, a problem arises in presenting a philosophy that is skewed toward Christian eschatological and religious thinking. Philosophy, as the pursuit of truth and of wisdom about the Being of beings, and about the freedom of human beings, should appeal also to atheists and to members of all faiths.

Berdyaev does not seem to have cared. Islam, for instance, seems beyond the horizon of his thinking; we have not found more than a reference here and there to this world religion in his writings. Thus, to put it lightly, we find problems with Berdyaev's philosophy of religion, his philosophy of history, and his eschatology. In addition, we have found that many of Berdyaev's statements on love between true lovers, especially his remarks on intimate physical and sexual love between lovers, to be untenable, and frequently false.

Our disagreements with some of Berdyaev's major ideas do not diminish our great appreciation of the profundity of some of his insights and ideas in other realms. For instance, we have learned much from one of

Berdyaev's most prominent philosophical concerns: the developing of a free, creative personality. In his discussions on human freedom, creativity, and personality, Berdyaev grasped himself as an existentialist philosopher; he often mentions that his thinking is in the tradition of Nietzsche and of Kierkegaard. Hence, his thinking is not phenomenological, in the sense that Edmund Husserl, and his many followers, used the word "phenomenology." Indeed, Berdyaev criticized Husserl's writings on phenomenology, and also the writings of those existentialists, such as Heidegger and Sartre, who learned from Husserl and who based much of their thinking on ideas central to Husserl's approach.

The struggle for freedom and creativity, and the difficult quest for personality, are themes that repeatedly appear in Berdyaev's many writings. We believe that Berdyaev's thinking on freedom, creativity, and the challenge of personality are helpful in seeing the faults in the works of sophistry that have been produced by many twentieth-century so-called artists. His thinking also proves significant in rejecting the superficiality and the sophistry of those many intellectuals, among them journalists, art historians, and art critics who support and promote these works of fake art. In this chapter and in Chapter Six, we concentrate on a few of the insights that appear in Berdyaev's book *Slavery and Freedom*. The book describes many of the ways, especially those prevalent in contemporary society, by which persons become enslaved to unworthy lures, and, consequently, forfeit their freedom, their creativity, and their quest for personality.

What is personality, according to Berdyaev? How does a person strive to live his or her freedom and creativity in a worthy manner, and thus live fully one's personality? Berdyaev cautions us that the human being is a riddle in the world:

> Man is a riddle in the world, and it may be the greatest riddle. Man is a riddle not because he is an animal, not because he is a social being, not as a part of nature and society. It is as a person that he is a riddle — just that precisely; it is because he possesses personality.[2]

Without going further, we can ask: Has any one of the works by the producers of fake art whom we have attacked in previous chapters — say, Frank Stella, Jackson Pollock, Jasper Johns, Carl Andre, Roy Lichtenstein, Piet Mondrian, or Ben Nicholson — any relation to the riddle that emerges because human beings possess personality? As an initial response, the answer is: No!

If we look at these works of fake art, and endeavor to relate them to the riddle of being a person who possesses personality, we soon reach the conclusion that these works tell us nothing about this riddle. In relation to the riddle of being a person, these works are vacuous and sterile. Learning from

Berdyaev, we shall soon explain that works of so-called art that do not relate to the riddle of being a person who possesses personality are necessarily sophistry.

In contrast to the works of the producers of sophistry, you only need to look at Rembrandt's self-portraits, or at Paul Cézanne's portraits of his wife, or at Leonardo da Vinci's famous painting, "Mona Lisa," to be confronted with works of art that relate to the riddle of being a person who possesses personality. But, let us not hasten. We prefer to proceed slowly. Hence, in the three chapters of this book in which we deal with Berdyaev's thinking, we wish to present carefully, albeit very briefly, some of the thoughts that Berdyaev formulated about the riddle of personality, and how these thoughts condemn the works of sophistry that have flourished in twentieth-century art.

The human entity, according to Berdyaev, is a polarized being. A person is capable of striving for a higher vocation, for perfecting his or her way of being while striving for things that are worthy such as justice. But a person is also capable of much cruelty, of performing terrible evils, and of an abominable egoism — attitudes and behaviors which destroy a person's personality. The consciousness that each human being has of personality is what allows and encourages a person to speak of and to strive to attain a higher vocation in life and, perhaps, to strive for excellence, for truth, for justice, and for a perfected existence. Among all the beings in the world, only human beings are endowed with the possibility of developing their personality. This possibility, according to Berdyaev, is the key to spiritual existence.

But what does a person do when he or she strives to develop his or her personality? Here are three quite general possible answers that emerge from Berdyaev's writings. A striving to develop your personality often means spiritually perfecting your existence. Such a striving can also mean answering, with your entire being, the call to a higher vocation which you may hear. This call may encourage you to dedicate your life, say, to the pursuit of beauty, or to the realization of justice, or to unconcealing truth, or to acquiring knowledge, or to attaining wisdom. It can also mean struggling, in your day-today existence, to live a free, creative life. The answers are not mutually exclusive; indeed, often they overlap.

Berdyaev immediately and repeatedly points out that we cannot compare personality to any other being that exists in the world. Personality is definitely not an object. Nor can we reduce personality to psychological or to biological components, such as desires, wishes, drives, lusts, or instincts. Nor is personality a result of social existence, because society objectifies human existence, and, usually, does not encourage people to live as personalities. Unfortunately, many people placidly accept these demands of society; they live all their lives engaged in fulfilling the objectivized requirements put forward by their society without ever establishing and living their own personality.

A engaging social life, or an ambitious political life will often be totally devoid of relating to others as persons with a personality. Such a mode of existence is spiritually sterile, albeit it will frequently occur in affluent, and so-called noble society, as Marcel Proust has brilliantly shown in *Remembrance of Things Past*.[3] You can also find descriptions of the lack of personality in so-called aristocratic society, and in many pseudo-intellectual bourgeois circles in society, in the writings of Lev Tolstoy and Henrik Ibsen, whose originality and insights Berdyaev admired and frequently mentioned.

Nor, Berdyaev adds, can we argue that personality is an element which came into being during the evolution of the biological beings in the world, which culminated in human beings. It is not difficult to clarify why personality is not linked to the accepted theories of evolution. Personality has no precedent or forerunner in the biological or physical beings that surround us. Furthermore, the current theories of evolution are based on a process whereby organisms perfect, by random mutation, their survival techniques, and with them, their own being. Such a process has nothing to do with the emergence of personality. Indeed, personality has nothing to do with survival techniques.

Berdyaev would probably suggest that a free, creative person will often scorn survival techniques. Such is frequently true. Usually, a person who undertakes the ongoing quest for personality, which frequently includes the striving to perfect his or her existence, or the struggle for justice, or the creation and appreciation of works of beauty, or the search for wisdom is hardly concerned with his or her survival. Socrates is a vivid and inspiring example of such a person, who daily sought wisdom; he also strove to develop his personality in light of the knowledge and wisdom that had become unconcealed during his inquiries. Such a person's major concern is to live freely and creatively, and not to be enslaved to some of the many lures with which society and life confront him or her. Thus, striving to be a personality requires courage and openness to truth. We can sense here an echo of Nietzsche's thinking on the struggle to be creative, especially as expressed in *Thus Spoke Zarathustra*,[4] an echo which Berdyaev would acknowledge.

Since personality cannot be reduced or explained by other terms or events, Berdyaev holds that the fact that a person can possess personality is an exciting and inspiring riddle. He adds: "Personality is a break through, a breaking in upon this world; it is an introduction of something new."[5]

We can already see that Berdyaev's term, "personality," can include a challenge which faces every person. It is a complex and difficult challenge. One reason for the complexity and difficulty is that the human being who possesses personality is a riddle. Berdyaev explains that the person who possesses personality is not a monad among other monads, since monads, according to Leibniz's definition, are essentially isolated; instead, the person with personality is a microcosm that, at times, strives to relate as a whole being to other persons who can be personalities. The person with personality will also endeavor to relate to the infinite beyond him or her.

Berdyaev indicates that, in responding to the call of personality, there is a fundamental paradox. In order to strive to be a personality, to enhance and enrich yourself as a free and creative being, to express yourself creatively and freely, to relate as a whole being to other persons and to other beings which you may encounter, you must already exist as a personality. Put differently, personality emerges when a person acts as a whole, but for that to happen, there must be a subject, an unique person, who feels that he or she is called upon to relate as a whole. And this subject, this person, must decide to construct oneself as a personality who can, at times, relate as a whole being.

Relating as a whole being, it should be clear, excludes all manipulation of other persons, which means that it excludes using other persons as a means to your own ends. But since each person exists in a world and in a society that is very much governed by means and ends, relating as a whole being is very difficult. Whether we like it or not we often relate to other human beings as means to further our own ends. Hence, relating as a whole being is a mode of existence to which the person should strive in daily encounters.

In this striving to live the mode of existence of wholeness, each person attempts to live and to create his or her unique personality. Berdyaev explains that realizing your unique personality is a creative act, because each personality is irrepeatable; it is different from all other personalities that ever existed. Put succinctly, the developing of your personality is a creative victory against those many forces that exist in society, and in the world, which strive to and can often objectify and enslave each person and ruin his or her personality.

On the basis of Berdyaev's tenet that personality is the source of spiritual existence, we believe a rather simple proposition to be true. A person encountering a beautiful painting or a beautiful sculpture or a beautiful work of architecture frequently will find that the painting or the sculpture or the work of architecture relates to his or her unique irrepeatable personality. Conversely, when a person encounters a painting or a sculpture or a work of architecture and discovers that it does not, and cannot relate to his or her unique irrepeatable personality, usually the painting or the sculpture or the building is not beautiful. Furthermore, we hold that when a person meets a painting or sculpture or building that does not and cannot relate to his or her personality, that painting or sculpture or building is not a work of art. It is either an ugly work, or a spiritually vacuous painting or sculpture or building, or an installation which is not beautiful, or any other perversion from the realm of genuine art. In short, works of sophistry do not relate to the personality of the observer.

Someone may ask: what is the secret by which a beautiful work of art relates to the personality of the observer? In this book we only will give partial answers to this question — for many reasons. At present, we mention two of these reasons. First, we accept Berdyaev's statement that the human being who possesses personality is a riddle; therefore, a full answer is well nigh impossible, since the riddle of personality cannot be fully solved. Second, we agree with Plato, who showed in *Greater Hippias*, that a full definition of the beautiful is very difficult, if not impossible to formulate. Thus, the secret by which a beautiful work relates to personality is also very difficult to formulate.

We will, however, present an initial, partial answer, to the above question. Our answer is based on the description that we gave of the ways a person may respond to the challenge of personality.

For a work of art to be able to relate to the personality of an observer, it must relate to those three possibilities which face a person who strives to develop his or her personality. Thus, the work of art that relates to personality should be able to enrich a person's endeavors to perfect his or her existence; in the context of our discussion such can occur, say, by exposing the person to beauty and to the unconcealing of truth. Perhaps, by such an exposure, the work of art will reveal to the observing person some of his or her possibilities and responsibilities in the world. In great portraits, say by Velázquez, the observer can also be exposed to the personality, or to the lack of personality, of the person whose portrait has been painted by the painter. We hold it quite true to state that the great portrait unconceals truths about the personality and the life of the person who was painted.

In addition, the work of art that appeals to personality should encourage a person who wishes to respond to the call of a higher vocation; among the higher vocations that we have mentioned are the pursuit of justice, or the creation of beauty, or the unconcealing of truth, or the striving to attain knowledge and wisdom. Finally, a beautiful work of art may encourage the person relating to it to live a free and creative existence. One manner by which a work of art encourages persons is by showing him or her that freedom and creativity can bring forth enhancing gifts for humankind, among them, great works of art, works that are beautiful and that unconceal truth.

We want to add an example that will support our partial answer to the above question: "What is the secret by which a beautiful work of art relates to the personality of the observer?" For that, we shall consider a beautiful painting and suggest how it relates to the personality of the observer. The painting we have in mind was painted by the Belgian artist, James Ensor, who lived from 1860 until 1949. Although James Ensor was a contemporary of some of the producers of fake art whose works we have condemned and rejected — for instance, Piet Mondrian (1872-1944) — his many paintings are not sophistry. It seems that Ensor was never influenced by the producers of sophistry in twentieth-century art and by the various art movements that encouraged such sophistry, say, Dada, Abstraction, Surrealism, Minimalism.

The painting we chose, as exemplifying our answer to the above question, is called "Ensor Surrounded by Masks"; it was painted by James Ensor in 1899. "Ensor Surrounded by Masks" was exhibited in 1999, in a large retrospect of Ensor's art commemorating the 50th anniversary of his death, in the Royal Museum of Fine Art of Belgium, in Brussels. We were fortunate to see the exhibition, in which scores of Ensors's paintings and drawings were displayed. The painting, "Ensor Surrounded by Masks," also adorns the cover of the catalogue that was published to commemorate this retrospect of Ensor's art, and includes all the paintings exhibited in the exhibition in Brussels.[6]

As the name "Ensor Surrounded by Masks" may suggest, close to the middle of the canvas is a self portrait of the painter, and around the portrait are painted a few dozen masks. The observer immediately perceives the distinction between the face of a live human being, in this case the face of James Ensor himself, who is endowed with the challenge of personality, and the dozens of masks of human beings whose features are frozen, and, at times, distorted. Immediately, you perceive that these masks have no relationship to the riddle of personality.

The painting can, therefore, bring the observer to wonder on the difference between a life in which you live as a person and strive to develop your personality — a striving in which you may respond to the call of a vocation — and a life in which you live hidden behind a mask, with almost no freedom and creativity, and no development of your personality. In addition, as observer, you may wonder as to some of the distortions of your being and some of the personal enslavements that you may embrace when you live hidden behind a mask. Are not these personal enslavements and distortions of your existence, that you may daily embrace, finally etched into your mask?

"Ensor Surrounded by Masks" also seems an apt portrait of much that occurs in contemporary society. As such, the painting unconceals many truths that Berdyaev taught us. Is it not true, as Berdyaev's discussion intimates, and as Ensor's beautiful painting reveals, that a free creative person, who strives to respond to the challenge of personality, frequently is surrounded by many dozens of people who live their entire life hidden behind a mask? Does not such a continual living behind a mask express the enslavement and distorted mode of existence of many people? Does not living behind a mask also imply an enslavement of each person's freedom and a rejection of his or her creativity? Does not living behind a mask also imply a firm rejection of the enhancement and the worthy life that may be attained by striving to be a personality? Our answer to these four questions is: Yes.

One reason that "Ensor Surrounded by Masks" is beautiful, is that the personality of the painter emerges, albeit as a riddle, in Ensor's self-portrait. Like other great self-portraits, say, those by Rembrandt and Van Gogh, the observer senses that Ensor's face in the painting partially discloses — or to borrow a word from Heidegger, partially unconceals — his personality. Put differently, while looking at the self-portrait of Ensor, you sense that you are standing before a portrait of a fellow person who has a complex personal story to relate, who has struggled with the riddle of his possessing a personality. Thus, when encountering Ensor's self-portrait, or the self-portraits of Rembrandt and Van Gogh, the observer recognizes that he or she is in the presence of a portrait of a person who struggled for spirituality.

In reality, Ensor's face in the self-portrait is not very different from the painting of a mask; its features are frozen, as are the features of Rembrandt's and Van Gogh's self-portraits. Yet the throb of life, the difficulties of struggling for spirituality, and the responding to the call to be a personality are evident in the face of all of these self-portraits. In contrast, no throb of life, no spirituality, and no struggle for freedom and creativity can be discerned in any mask, including the masks that surround the self-portrait of Ensor. Thus, in his painting, "Ensor Surrounded by Masks," Ensor disclosed an important truth: the distinction between living as a personality, and living as a mask — without undertaking the attempt to be a personality — frequently can be seen in a person's face.

From our brief description, it is not difficult to conclude that Ensor's painting relates, at least partially, to the three components of the struggle for personality mentioned above. Formulating these simple conclusions would be repetitious. Conversely, in works of fake art, such as Jasper Johns's paintings of the American map and flag and of targets, Frank Stella's painting "New Madrid," Piet Mondrian's colored patterns, Roy Lichtenstein's enlarged comics, Carl Andre's red cedar modules, or in Minimalist paintings, there is no hint of the attempt or the longing to respond to the call of personality. There cannot be. These works of sophistry, that are not beautiful, and whose producers made no claim to their being beautiful, are shallow expressions of alienation from the quest for personality. Consequently, these works are alienated from the live person observing them, who may wish to respond to the call of personality, and live as a spiritual being.

Our description here is ontological. Works of fake art do not relate to what Berdyaev calls the riddle of being a person and possessing personality. Nor have those critics, historians, and journalists, who admire and extol the works of Mondrian, Pollock, Stella, Nicholson, Rothko, Segal, Andre, and of many other producers of sophistry in twentieth-century art, ever suggested that the works which they are praising relate to the riddle of being a person and possessing personality. This fact might be an additional reason for the indifference that emanates from the works of fake art, an indifference which we discussed in Chapter Four. The persons observing works of fake art in a museum or gallery probably sense intuitively that these paintings, sculptures, and installations are vacuous and totally indifferent to their personality.

At this juncture, someone may bring up an important question for the history of comparative art. In many paintings painted by artists from Japan, China, and other countries of the Far East, the faces of the persons in the painting frequently resemble masks. A person who has looked carefully at art from the Far East might add: From my limited experience such a painting of masks, and not faces which disclose what you call personality, seems to have been the tradition in much Japanese, Chinese, and other Far East paintings. Would you suggest that many of these paintings from Japan, China, and other countries of the Far East are alienated from the challenge of personality?

Our personal answer is a qualified: Yes. These paintings are frequently alienated from the challenge of personality for the simple reason that masks conceal the personality of the person. Hence, the challenge of personality is frequently lacking in paintings of the Far East.

We should add, however, that art, painting, and sculpture in the Far East is not uniform. We have seen beautiful Indian sculptures and some lovely Chinese ceramics and other works of art that do respond to the observer who wishes to undertake the challenge of personality. At this point, we prefer to leave the question open. Providing even a partial answer to this question would take us much too far afield.

Berdyaev states: "Personality is a subject, and not an object among other objects...."[7] He adds that one of the most prominent dangers, which lurk in the immediate neighborhood of a person who wishes to live as a personality, is grasping oneself as an object among other objects. The viewing of personality as an object, however, has become common with the spreading influence of science. What is more, the social or behavioral sciences, among them sociology, psychology, anthropology, political science, and economics almost always relate to the person as an object, hardly ever as a personality.[8]

Berdyaev agrees that society and nature are elementary necessities for a person to exist and for personality to come into being. But, he adds, for your personality to begin to emerge you must emancipate yourself from dependence upon the persistent objectification of persons that prevails in society, in the state, and in various manifestations of these two social forms, for instance, in your relations with your ethnic community or your political party.

The reason that, without such an emancipation, you will find it difficult to respond to the challenge of personality is quite evident. Your society, your state, your ethnic community, and your political party perceive you and relate to you as an object that exists among many other similar objects. These social institutions, and their many representatives that confront you and relate to you, attempt to determine your way of life on the basis of external relations and external demands that have nothing to do with your inwardness and your unique irrepeatable personality. To use a slang-like phrase: Most often ethnic, social, and political institutions, and their bureaucrats and representatives, couldn't care less about your personality.

Every person who has struggled to develop his or her personality knows that his or her unique irrepeatable personality will only come into being on the basis of internal decisions and personal determinations. He or she also know well that, quite frequently, these personal decisions and determinations must oppose many of the external demands and requirements posed by the society, by the state, and by the community to which the person belongs. The person who responds to the call of personality also perceives that those external demands and requirements, which he or she must reject, are adhered to by many members of his or her community, society, and state. He or she learns, quite quickly, that many of these members of society or of the state will reject any person who questions the broadly accepted determinations and demands of these social and political institutions.

Hence, every person should know that responding to the challenge of personality very often entails undergoing loneliness, alienation, and personal suffering. It can imply being personally rejected by that person's community or being ostrasized and condemned by his or her immediate milieu. Think of Socrates. Despite all of this, and perhaps because of it, responding to the call of personality also can bring moments of good faith, of genuine comradeship, of true love and of great joy. It is, therefore, not surprising to find Berdyaev repeatedly writing statements such as "Personality as an existential centre, presupposes capacity to feel suffering and joy."[9]

We can now ask a simple question. What is the difference between an advertisement or a slogan — say, an advertisement for Campbell's Soup, or a slogan that encourages respect for the flag of the United States — and a great work of twentieth-century art, say, a painting by Picasso, Matisse, or Balthus?

One answer comes to mind immediately. An advertisement and a slogan belong solely to the realm of objectivization. Advertisements and slogans are objects among other objects. They are means to a specific end. Their primary goal is to seduce us to accept their statements, and to succumb to their lure. Hence, the advertisement and the slogan relate to the person who observes them or listens to them as if he or she were an object among other alienated objects. Furthermore, an advertisement or a slogan may arouse curiosity, or perhaps even admiration at its being a clever manner of expression. But neither the advertisement nor the slogan arouses wonder, which is a response of a person's entire being.

Let us repeat. The goal of the advertisement is to lure, and perhaps to shock persons who encounter it; its overall goal is to seduce its observers or listeners to purchase the product that is being advertised, or to support the cause that is dear to the advertiser.

In contrast, a great work of art was created so as to appeal and relate to the personality of a person — and it does not matter whether or not the artist recognizes these qualities in the work that he or she created. Put succinctly, a person encountering a great work of art, say, Tintoretto's "The Crucifixion," which we discuss in Chapter Ten, may find that the work of art relates to him or her as a person who can attempt to live as a free, creative personality. It also opens the observer to the possibility of responding to the call of personality by showing him or her that the pursuit of excellence, which is central to living as a personality, can bring forth beauty and truth. A great work of art, say, Michelangelo's painting of the ceiling of the Sistine Chapel, or his sculpture, "David," arouses our wonder. We can safely assume that Michelangelo did not paint that ceiling or sculpt that sculpture in order to arouse curiosity or to seduce us to admire his cleverness, or to convince us to purchase a product or support a cause.

It is not difficult to perceive that the works of fake art which we reject and attack — produced by Warhol, Johns, Stella, Mondrian, Miro, Nicholson, and many others — are each much more similar to advertisements and to slogans than to the works of art of Picasso, Matisse, and Balthus. The reason is simple. The works of fake art do not relate to the person as a being who possesses personality; they ignore the riddle of personality. In contrast, the great works of Picasso, Matisse, and Balthus arouse our wonder and do relate to us observers as persons who possess personality. The conclusion is quite sad. The work of fake art is an object among other objects; as such it does not relate to the personality of the observer of the work. If it does relate to the observer, it suggests that the observer is also an object among other objects. This insidious reign of objectivity, this degradement of spiritual possibilities into mere objective beings, Berdyaev stresses, destroys personality and spirituality.

As already explained, especially in the sections where we learned from Plato's *Sophist*, when a work of fake art relates to a person observing it as an object among other objects, the work may only succeed in attracting his or her attention by means of seduction. Again, advertisements and jingoist slogans come to mind. Advertisements and jingoist slogans are evidently a manner of seducing the person seeing the advertisement or hearing the slogan to purchase or to relate favorably to a particular object or group of objects. Quite often the two realms blend, and an advertiser may seek a slogan, or in the terms of the advertising business, a jingle, that catches the imagination of the people whom the advertiser wishes to seduce. In addition, a government may support, say, a jingoist appeal to its citizens and residents, with advertisements. In many works of fake art, you will also find a similar blending of slogans and advertisement.

This discussion leads us to an ontological conclusion. In their essence, as phenomenal exhibited in museums and in many galleries, many works of sophistry in twentieth-century art are frequently closer to advertisements and to slogans than to genuine art.

One way by which producers of works of sophistry in twentieth-century art can concentrate on developing manners of seducing the observers of their works, while eluding the challenge of personality, is by never painting portraits. After all, a portrait, in order to be beautiful and great, or, at least, worthy or informative, must give the observer a glimpse of the personality, the character, the depth, and the inwardness of the person whose portrait has been painted. But when you paint merely abstract patterns — as Frank Stella, Ben Nicholson, Piet Mondrian, Jackson Pollock, Vasili Kandinsky, Clyfford Still, and many others have painted — there is no need to be aware of the riddle of any person or of the quest for personality.

This evasion of the challenge of painting portraits, which has become clearly visible in the many works of sophistry that invaded and became prominent in museums and in galleries in the past seven or eight decades, requires a short digression. Since the evasion of the challenge of painting portraits is a manner of eluding the call of personality, we believe the digression to be an apt way to complete this chapter.

The painter, Alice Neel (1900-1984), was exceptional in her concentration on painting portraits. Most of the years that she painted, however, were a period when trends such as Dada, Surrealism, Minimalism, Pop-Art, and Abstract Expressionism prevailed in twentieth-century art. Many of the people in these realms, who produced works of fake art, were having a field day. Consequently, a genuine artist, like Neel, who painted portraits, was considered unoriginal, not interesting, and not fitting the times. This shallow approach to art led to the fact that Neel's beautiful paintings were persistently ignored by administrators and curators of museums, and by art critics and journalists who deal with art. But that is another story.

Today we can state that Neel's moving portraits provide the observer with a glimpse into the spiritual life and the personality of the person whom Neel painted. It is, therefore, evident that her portraits, which disclose profound elements of the personality of the person who has been painted — and also provide hints about the riddle of that personality — frequently appeal to the personality of the observer.

Writing about Neel's work, and its place in twentieth-century painting, Patricia Hills observed:

> "The good painter must depict two principal things," said Leonardo da Vinci, "man and the concept of his mind." Modern artists are exhaustingly depicting the latter while largely ignoring the former. Outside of professional portraitists, who provide a service rather than create art, the portrait has almost disappeared among serious contemporary painters.[10]

Without examining whether da Vinci got it right in describing the good painter, or whether Patricia Hills is correct in stating that contemporary artists are only "depicting the concept of their minds" — whatever that phrase means — one major fact mentioned in the above citation is true. The portrait, as a work of creative painting, has disappeared in the entire realm of twentieth-century art that we have termed sophistry. The portrait did not disappear in the works of Picasso, Beckman, Ensor, Neel, Balthus, Derain, and many other genuine artists. These painters continued to paint beautiful portraits. For instance, Picasso's portrait of Gertrude Stein, which hangs in the Metropolitan Museum of Art in New York City, is a masterpiece. And Max Beckman's many self-portraits unconceal truths about his life, his sufferings, and his personality.

Why has it happened that not one of the producers of works of fake art whom we have attacked, and many others whom we did not mention — why have they not painted portraits? Why have they painted posters or, what should be termed, masks, when they painted persons — and not portraits? Using Berdyaev's terms, the answer is evident.

When painting a portrait, the good painter must relate to the riddle of the person who is being painted, which includes relating to his or her personality. Specifically, the painter must relate to the depth and the complexity of this riddle in the unique irrepeatable person whose portrait he or she is painting; furthermore, the personality of the person must, somehow, be present in the portrait. Put differently, a good portrait will never depict the person who is being painted merely as an object among other objects. Instead, the good portrait brings us into the presence of a live person to whom we can relate; it brings us into the presence of a personality, as expressed through the person's face and body. When encountering a good portrait, the observer sees in the portrait a person with a personality.

From their many works, we can conclude that the challenge of painting the portrait of a person which will reveal his or her personality is beyond the horizon of Jackson Pollock, Roy Lichtenstein, Clyfford Still, Jasper Johns, Ben Nicholson, Joan Miro, and most other famous people who produced works of sophistry. In the works of these famous producers of sophistry, you do not even comprehend the possibility of such a challenge. Painting a portrait of a person with personality is also beyond the horizon of many hundreds of other producers of works of fake art, whose works clutter museums and hang in galleries.

By persistently refraining from painting portraits, all of these producers of fake art flee from coping with the riddle of personality and its worthy challenge. Since their works are mere sophistry, since they present the observer with uninspiring paintings and sculptures – that seemingly exist as objects among other objects — at most, these works may arouse curiosity or interest. They never arouse the wonder that, according to Plato, may lead to wisdom. These works of fake art will never establish relations with their observers as whole persons. Like the sophists whom Plato repeatedly rejected, the works of these producers of fake art cannot relate to free, creative, thinking persons. Also, their works do not relate to truth or unconceal truth. Since many of these works only express the vacuity of abstraction, and the emptiness that accompanies objectivization of persons, they cannot relate to personality.

Finally, to end this digression, and this chapter, we again mention one sad result of the flight of the painters, who are sophists, from the challenge of portrait painting. By exhibiting the shallow works of these so-called artists, works that relate to the observer as an object among other objects, works that exude an aura of sterility, and often of inanity, museums have become impoverished. One reason for this widespread impoverishment is that many museums are full of inane works of sophistry that do not at all relate to the person who possesses personality, and to the riddle of personality.

Someone may respond: Why do you repeatedly call the works that you brand sophistry inane? In the next chapter, with the help of Berdyaev's thinking, we answer this question, and provide a pertinent example of accepted inanity in twentieth-century art.

Six

BERDYAEV'S PERSONALISM VERSUS EGOCENTRICISM IN ART

Berdyaev calls his philosophical thinking: Personalism. He wishes to include in Personalism all thinking that discusses the challenge of personality, and the significance of personality. Personalism also repeatedly points in detail to the possibility, that exists for each person, to develop his or her personality, and to respond to the challenge of living as a personality. Berdyaev explains that

> it [Personalism] understands personality in a sense that is profoundly antithetic to egoism. Egoism destroys personality. Egocentric self-containment and concentration upon the self is original sin, which prevents the realization of the full life of personality and hinders its strength from becoming effective.[1]

Although we believe that Berdyaev's linking of egocentric self-containment to original sin, can be partially justified, explaining this partial justification is beyond the scope of our present discussion. However, even without the concept of original sin, we believe that Berdyaev is correct in pointing out that a person who lives daily engrossed in egocentric self-containment, and concentration upon the self "prevents the realization of the full life of [his or her] personality and hinders its strength of becoming effective."

Examples of Berdyaev's statement are not difficult to find, both in literature and in life. For a rather extreme literary example, consider King Richard III, in Shakespeare's play *The Life and Death of King Richard III*. It is not difficult to brand Richard III as an individual whose entire existence is directed toward evil deeds that will bring him to be crowned king of England and, later, to maintain his throne. His evil deeds realize and are expressions of Richard's "egocentric self-containment and concentration upon the self." Scholars have emphasized this point, albeit in slightly different language.

But many scholars who discuss Shakespeare's tragedy of King Richard III, have often overlooked a major point that also seems little noticed by viewers of the tragedy. Using Berdyaev's language, we would add that King Richard III has no personality beyond his evil egocentric obsessions. Nothing. His unabated egocentricism, and the many evil deeds that he performs to obtain the desires of this pernicious egocentricism, have strangled all remnants of Richard III's personality. Berdyaev might have added that, in discussions of this tragedy, it is most unfortunate that this self-strangling of his own personality, by the evil egocentric King Richard III, has been often ignored.

Berdyaev's statement that egocentric self containment is ruinous for a person's personality is not confined to well known examples, such as Shakespeare's King Richard III or, say, the historical example of Nero playing on his fiddle while Rome burned. Politics in the twentieth century brought many additional well known examples — from Stalin and Hitler to Franco and Pinochet — of leaders whose actions were at least as terrible as those of Shakespeare's Richard III. From our limited knowledge, the results for these wicked persons included a self-strangling of their own personality.

But there are also less famous examples of the self-strangling of personality, and of the ignoring the challenge of personality. The sensitive person will encounter such people in everyday life. For instance, a person who confines his or her existence to a single mood, or to a series of moods, without relating to what happens in the surrounding world, without relating to the Being of other persons, is also egocentric. We also reject as egocentric the justification proffered by many such persons that they are very sensitive, hence they are given to moods. In this context, consider a revealing citation from the writings of Søren Kierkegaard's fictional character, A, the spokesman in *Either/Or,* Volume 1.

We should remind the reader that Kierkegaard describes his narrator, A, as a committed aesthete, who attempts to develop a theory that justifies his sterile, non-spiritual, frequently utilitarian, highly egocentric approach to life, to other persons, and to art. A's description of himself, in a series of brief statements and telling anecdotes, opens the volume and exemplifies the way of life of the aesthete. A's statements and anecdotes also show how his egoistic self-containment ruins his personality. In one instance, A reveals that he is often given to a single mood. Listen to A's confession on this matter, which has enlightening implications for sophistry in twentieth-century art.

> The result of my life is simply nothing, a mood, a single
> color. My result is like the painting of the artist who was
> to paint a picture of the Israelites crossing the Red Sea.
> To this end he painted the whole wall red, explaining that
> the Israelites had already crossed over, and that the
> Egyptians were drowned.[2]

Abandon, for a moment, Berdyaev's tenet about egoism. Think about the movement of Minimalist painting, that emerged in the mid-twentieth century, and was applauded by a host of art critics, journalists, and thinkers on art. Minimalism was crowned as a most significant movement in abstract painting. The famous art historian, Herbert Read, in his book, *A Concise History of Modern Painting*, defined Minimalist works as paintings with "minimal color and minimal image."[3] This definition, which seems to have been broadly accepted by other historians, critics, and lay persons, is destructive of painting and of sculpture, which, since their inception, have dealt with color and image. We return to this topic in the next chapter.

If we look again at the above citation from *Either/Or,* Volume 1, can we not say that, probably, all twentieth century Minimalist paintings resemble the picture of the Israelites crossing the Red Sea that Kierkegaard considers ludicrous, and yes, stupid? Our answer is: Yes. Would it be totally out of order, according to Kierkegaard and to our simple intuitions and common sense, to call such paintings inane?

Remember that Kierkegaard wrote the above lines a century before the Minimalist painters began to exhibit their barren, one-mood, one-color paintings, which are extreme examples of sophistry, and which can today be found hanging in galleries and museums around the world. Yet Kierkegaard's short anecdote shows what is wrong with such paintings. Since they appeal to a single mood, and reject the complexity of human existence, they are not beautiful and do not unconceal truth. They have no story to tell, they have no relation to reality, or to the existence of live persons. Perhaps, as some of the producers of these works of fake art suggest, Minimalist paintings are merely an attempt to express a mood without relating it to persons or to objects in the surrounding world. In a word, Minimalist paintings express egoistic self-containment, nothing more. As Marc, in Reza's play, *Art,* immediately discerns, when he confronts Serge's totally white painting, Minimalist paintings are not works of art. As mentioned, he calls the painting "shit."

The result is quite evident when you think about the implications arising from the above citation and the challenge of personality. Minimalist paintings are vacuous, banal, uninspiring, alienating. They have nothing to convey. They exude an aura of sterility and impotence in relation to the difficult struggles you will face if you strive to relate spiritually to the world that we all share. These struggles require that you respond to the challenge of personality, and to the complex situation in which you find yourself in the world. Minimalist paintings, therefore, are vivid examples of a radical and destructive sophistry that emerged in twentieth-century art. They are also inane.

Using Berdyaev's language, we hold that all Minimalist paintings are clear examples of "egocentric self containment and concentration upon the self." They are all spiritually barren. They are pictorial expressions of a spiritual wasteland; they testify to a tendency among some intellectuals to accept every inanity as a possible work of art. Many such inanities have invaded and become quite acceptable in contemporary art, as again, the play, *Art,* reveals. We should add that, in our humble view, Minimalist paintings are extreme examples of the barrenness and vacuousness of all twentieth-century works of fake art.

At times fiction supports fact, however ludicrous and inane that fiction may be. In 1966-1967, one hundred and eleven years after Kierkegaard died, Barnett Newman exhibited a large Minimalist painting in which he painted the whole canvas red. The only difference between Newman's painting and the ludicrous work described by Kierkegaard's fictional narrator, A, is that in Newman's painting there is a very thin left margin painted yellow, and bit broader right margin painted blue. Newman called his painting, which is photographed in Herbert Read's above-mentioned book, "Who's Afraid of Red, Yellow, and Blue III?"[4]

Evidently, the answer to the provocative, or perhaps teasing, question that titles Newman's Minimalist painting is that Barnett Newman is not afraid of Red, Yellow, and Blue III. Moreover, this lack of fear from Red, Yellow, and Blue III, seems to profoundly express Newman's being, otherwise why paint an entire canvass which expresses this remarkable question. Indeed, Newman's firm bravery and heroic courage, in face of the adverse and frightful effects that Red, Yellow, and Blue III can bring about, is what Newman's painting supposedly conveys. How perverse, and yes, how egocentric.

Newman's painting is, of course, a foolish work of sophistry. Yet let us look closer at the fact that this work of sophistry, this work of fake art, perfectly fits Kierkegaard's deriding description of the painting: "the Israelites crossing the Red Sea." The result, as Kierkegaard indicates in the above citation, is that Newman's painting is nothing, a single mood, a single color. The painting is spiritually vacuous. We repeat: It is an inanity. Barnett Newman's "Who's Afraid of Red, Yellow, and Blue III" is barren and impotent like the soul of Kierkegaard's clever and seductive aesthete, the immoral narrator, A. Would it be unfair to assume that Newman's soul resembles the barren soul of the clever seductive aesthete whom Kierkegaard describes and fiercely rejects? Perhaps.

Unfortunately, when he turns to writing and to explaining his views, Barnett Newman gives us no alternative but to view him as a shallow supercilious sophist. Consider two citations from an essay he authored and that he had the chutzpah to call "The Sublime is Now." The essay was published in 1948.

> The impulse of modern art was this impulse to destroy beauty.[5]
> I believe that here in America, free from the weight of European culture, we are finding the answer [to how to paint the sublime] by completely denying that art has any concern with the problem of beauty and where to find it.[6]

Without fully responding to Newman's bland egocentricism, revolting superciliousness, and chutzpah, it is evident that in his essay, "The Sublime is Now," he has divorced his and his colleague's so-called art from beauty and from the human longing for beauty. He has stated that he and his colleagues can paint the sublime without "any concern with the problem of beauty and where to find it." To attain that "worthy goal," the only matter that concerns Newman is that art should relate to the "absolute emotions."[7]

Kierkegaard's fictional figure, A, would embrace this fellow aesthete and sophist to his heart. From his paintings and writings, we can see that Newman enjoys living and expressing what he terms "absolute emotions," which are quite undistiguishable from A's frequently living a single mood. A's continual delight in playing with his own emotions and moods fits well with Newman's blunt egocentricism. However, as Kierkegaard stated and showed, no worthy art and no possibility of relating to the personality of a fellow human being can emerge from such a vacuous, egocentric, destructive approach.

As a corollary, a telling insight emerges from Barnett Newman's stupidities. We have here encountered an instant that justifies the popular saying: It is but one step from the sublime to the ridiculous. Barnett Newman may have believed that he searched for and found the sublime. But both the canvasses that he produced and labeled as art, and the essay that he wrote are ridiculous!

The person is a mystery, Berdyaev states, because he or she can attain personality; but, Berdyaev also shows that personality itself is a complex mystery. As Kierkegaard indicated, trying to reduce the complex mystery of personality to a single mood, is like trying to reduce complex mystery of creating a beautiful, or even a sublime painting, such as Michelangelo's ceiling of the Sistine Chapel, to smearing a single color on a canvas. Such an approach, Kierkegaard's writings suggest, is not only ludicrous, it is stupid and ruinous of a person's spiritual existence. Such an impoverishing reduction of the complexity of personality, and of genuine art, which is one of the worthy and creative expressions of personality, is among the worst manifestations and results of the triumph of sophistry in much of twentieth-century art.

Learning from Kierkegaard and from Berdyaev, we believe that the opposite is also the case. When a person, for instance, Barnett Newman, suggests that his painting of almost an entire canvas with red is a work of art, his work is not only an exercise in sophistry and in bad faith. Newman is not only attempting to deceive us and himself. Much more is at stake. Newman's perverse canvas, and his chutzpadic explanations of his approach, constitute an attempt to destroy personality and to undermine the essence and the origin of the work of art. This destruction comes about because Newman's work of sophistry, and his supercilious writings that attempt to justify his work of sophistry, reject any relationship to other persons, to beauty, to truth, to personality. They are egocentric and, at times, border on the autistic. We repeat: the painting "Who's Afraid of Red, Yellow, and Blue III?" is stupid. It is an extreme expression of egoistic self-containment, and therefore it is destructive of human spirituality.

To recapitulate the major points that we have presented in these two chapters, Berdyaev holds that responding to the challenge of personality is the viaticum of a worthy human existence. In order to live as a personality, a person must daily struggle to be free and creative, and to relate as a whole being to other persons as personalities, as whole beings with whom one shares the world. Great works of art, say, beautiful paintings by Tintoretto, or by Vermeer, or by Neel relate to and appeal to a person's personality, to his or her attempts to live as a free person and be creative. Great paintings also appeal to a person's longing for beauty and search for truth.

Great contemporary art, such as many paintings by Ensor, Picasso, and Matisse, can support and perhaps inspire a person who wishes to respond to the challenge of personality, and relate to the riddle of personality. As some of the superb paintings of Ensor, Picasso, and Matisse reveal, to support and inspire the challenge of personality, great art must be, in the words of Berdyaev cited above, "profoundly antithetic to egoism."

Twentieth-century works of sophistry in the visual arts have no relation to the call of personality or to the riddle of personality. These works of sophistry are spiritually barren, and hence inane; quite often these works exude an aura of sterility, impotence, egocentricism, and yes, deceit. These works of fake art do not appeal to a person's struggle for freedom and creativity. They seem to reject a person's longing for beauty and for truth, which can enhance one's personality. One major reason for the wasteland produced by the works of sophistry in twentieth-century art is that the egoistic and egocentric tendencies evident in all the works of fake art reject personality, and relate to persons as mere objects among other objects. Another reason is that works of fake art are essentially superficial.

What do we mean by superficiality in works of art? In Chapter Four, we have shown that works of fake art are indifferent to the observer and to what occurs in the world. Such indifference thrives on a superficial approach to what is happening in the world and on shallow relations with other persons. We can also answer that art that is not beautiful, does not unconceal truth, does not arouse wonder, and does not relate to the whole person or appeal to personality is superficial.

But we have more to say about the specific ways that superficiality emerges in many of the works of fake art that hang and stand in galleries and museums around the world. Hence, before continuing to present a few additional enlightening ideas and provoking thoughts that can be gleaned from Berdyaev's writings, we devote a short chapter to partially elucidate the superficiality that emerges in all of the works of sophistry in twentieth-century art.

Seven

SUPERFICIALITY IN TWENTIETH-CENTURY ART

> But is it not the fact that... art, the art of a
> Vintuel like that of an Elstir, makes the man
> himself apparent, rendering externally visible in
> the colours of the spectrum that intimate
> composition of those worlds which we call
> individual persons and which, without the aid of
> art, we should never know?[1]
>
> Marcel Proust

In the pages of *Remembrance of Things Past*, from which the above citation is taken, Marcel Proust is writing about genuine art. In Proust's work of fiction, Vintuel is a composer of beautiful musical compositions and Elstir is a painter of beautiful paintings. In the above citation, we could substitute names such as Stravinsky and Shostokovitch for that of Vintuel, and substitute names such as Cézanne and Matisse for that of Elstir — and the citation would be true. In contrast, if we place any of the names of the producers of works of fake art in the citation, instead of the names Vintuel and Elstir, Proust's statement becomes false.

Proust is pointing to one of the profound and inspiring roles of genuine art. He believes that art makes persons — with their complexity, with their intimate composition, with their personal world — externally visible. He adds, that without art, we perhaps should never know many persons, in the depth of their Being. We agree with Proust, and would add that, at times, only great works of art can help to present persons with this depth of Being.

Note that the citation from Proust supports, and also partially goes beyond, Heidegger's statements, that were presented in the first three chapters of this book. In those statements, Heidegger explains that the unconcealing of truth is one of the major origins of the work of art. The citation supports Heidegger's statements concerning the unconcealing of truth in a work of art in that it suggests that the work of art can make previously concealed components of a person's being "externally visible." It partially goes beyond Heidegger's thinking in suggesting that art can present an intimate composition of the very complex world of an individual person. Great portraits, say, by Velázquez, or by Tintoretto, or by Rembrandt, or by Cézanne, provide a vivid example of works of art that present an intimate composition of the complex world of an individual person. As we have already pointed out in Chapter Six, the twentieth-century producers of works of sophistry do not paint portraits.

Proust's question, which constitutes the citation, is an attempt, albeit a partial attempt, to fathom the profundity of great works of art. There is no need to undertake such an attempt with the works of sophistry in twentieth-century art. For the simple reason that these works are not at all profound. Their shallowness in relation to human endeavors and the depth and richness of human existence is obvious. For a person sensitive to great art, this shallowness may often scream out from the fake paintings or fake sculptures that he or she encounters in museums and galleries.

We want to be more specific. You immediately perceive that works of sophistry in twentieth century art make no attempt to relate to the intimate composition of the world of an individual person, and especially they do not relate to the person observing the work. For instance, Minimalist paintings, or Jackson Pollock's drip-paintings, or Roy Lichtenstein's enlarged comics, or Carl Andre's so-called sculptures of material standing there, or Andy Warhol's paintings of cans of Campbell's Soup, or Jasper Johns's paintings of targets or of American flags, and thousands of works like them, are totally alienated from the intimate composition of the Being of their observers. Nor do these works of sophistry relate to the Being of other beings which persons may encounter. Consequently, we view these works of fake art as bastions of superficiality.

How can a so-called work of art be a bastion of superficiality? Look, once again, at Herbert Read's already cited definition of Minimalism, as "minimal color and minimal image."[2] We already mentioned that this definition suggests that Minimalism destroys the essence of painting. For at least 25 centuries, all over the world, the essence of painting as an art included the attempt to create a work of beauty that would present images painted in the colors that would make the painting beautiful. The painting should also, as Proust suggested and as many painters believed, make truths about the human trials and travails upon earth externally visible. During these 25 centuries, a painting with minimal image and minimal color was, by definition, *not* a work of art.

We see no rhyme or reason to change this definition, which was accepted for centuries, and at least partially discloses the essence of painting as a work of art. Nor do we believe that there is any valid reason to reject the approach which holds that a painting that is genuine art should portray an image, painted in colors that make the painting beautiful. Nor have we found, among all the writers on contemporary art whom we have read, anyone who suggested a valid reason, or a convincing and enlightening argument which would justify changing the historically accepted definition. Therefore, we conclude that the producers of Minimalist paintings are sophists, who present non-being as if it had Being; they present a canvas without images and with minimal colors, which is not beautiful and does not unconceal truths, and they never suggest that it is beautiful or that it unconceals truths, as if it had the Being of a work of art.

We can now explain what constitutes a bastion of superficiality. It is a painting or a sculpture that masquerades as a work of art but unconceals no truth and is not beautiful; it is a painting or a sculpture that masquerades as a work of art and is so superficial that it does not relate to the personality, as Berdyaev understood this term, of the observer. A work of fake art that is a bastion of superficiality does not make externally visible the intimate composition of persons in the world, a quality of genuine art to which Proust points. Such a work will never arouse our wonder. What is there to wonder about when you encounter a weirdly painted target or flag of the United States, or a painted enlarged can of Campbell's Soup?

Here is an additional example. Joan Miro painted many works that are bastions of superficiality. For instance, his 1960 painting called "Woman in a Pretty Hat" is at the level of a painting painted by a talented third grade child. On a dirt-brown background Miro painted a brown oval outline of what seems to be a woman's face with two dark brown spots as eyes. On the top of that oval, an elongated dark brown form seems to be a brown hat. He added a small spot of green to the left of the so-called woman's face and a smaller spot of red to the right of the face. That's it.

Miro's painting is oversimplified and, yes, infantile. The painting discloses nothing about the intimate composition of the woman in a pretty hat. It is not beautiful, does not disclose personality or relate to the personality of the observer; the painting also unconceals no truth. All this does not matter to the ardent promoters of this work of sophistry. The writer of the guidebook of Fundacio Joan Miro in Barcelona, a gallery that is dedicated to the works of Miro in which "Woman in a Pretty Hat" hangs, praises this painting for its "sureness of gesture" and "subtlety."[3] Such non-committing empty words seem to be the only terms that can be mustered to praise a work of art that is empty, and a bastion of superficiality.

As Miro's "Woman in a Pretty Hat" indicates, the shallowness of a work of fake art also emerges because it has no presence from which truth and beauty emanate. Also, it has no relation to wisdom. When a painting or a sculpture or an installation that is a bastion of superficiality stands or hangs in a gallery — unfortunately, you will find thousands of these twentieth-century productions that are bastions of superficiality in museums and galleries all over the world — it establishes an island of alienation, insipidity, and shallowness. It exudes remoteness and indifference; it reveals nothing about the complexities of human existence, about excellence, or about the Being of beings. It is itself a Nothing.

But what if a painter wishes to describe human alienation and the widespread superficiality of human relations that currently prevail, and especially in those social and political realms where corporate capitalism has triumphed? Can someone create such paintings without his or her paintings becoming a bastion of superficiality? Our answer is resolute. Artists can paint great and beautiful paintings that are not superficial, and that unconceal truths about human alienation!

As an example to our answer, consider again the paintings of Edward Hopper, and especially, "Nighthawks," which we already mentioned in the Introduction, and in other chapters. We noted the moving beauty of "Nighthawks" as a work of art that describes human aloneness, loneliness, and alienation. If you look at Hopper's many exquisite and moving paintings, you will discover that "Nighthawks" is not alone in making human alienation and aloneness externally visible. Like "Nighthawks," many of Hopper's paintings are simply beautiful in addition to their depicting moments of human alienation and aloneness in contemporary life; frequently, they also reveal the superficiality that is repeatedly manifested in human relationships and interactions.

Note, however, that unlike the works of Minimalists, Installationists, and other producers of sophistry, Hopper's paintings are genuine works of art. When Hopper's paintings hang in a gallery, they do *not* establish islands of alienation and superficiality. Frequently, the opposite is the case. Hopper's paintings appeal to the observer; they may arouse the observer to think about his or her mode of existence in our contemporary world where corporate capitalism reigns and where alienation, aloneness, loneliness, and superficiality are accepted and common.

Furthermore, many of Hopper's paintings endeavor to establish what Martin Buber called a genuine dialogue with the observer.[4] They frequently call out to each observer to relate as a whole being, as a Thou, to each painting. If and when such a rare moment of grace, as Buber calls it, comes into being between the painting and the observer, the painting has become what he terms: a partner in dialogue. We will not develop Buber's ideas here. We can say that his thoughts add support to our attacks on sophistry in twentieth-century art; yet they only add marginally to the basis of our attacks on sophistry, which is founded on ideas of Heidegger and Berdyaev.

As already indicated, one of the things that a person who relates as a whole being will encounter in Hopper's paintings is the alienation, the aloneness, the loneliness, and the superficiality of human existence that prevails in contemporary society. Put differently, many of Hopper's paintings call out to and invite the observer to relate to each of them as a whole being, as a Thou, as what Berdyaev called a personality. And conversely, when a person relates as a whole being to one of Hopper's paintings, he or she will also perceive and behold the sad and haunting truths that the painting has unconcealed about alienation and aloneness in contemporary human existence, and about its ruinous effects on the quest for personality.

Since a Minimalist work, or Miro's "Woman in a Pretty Hat," or any other example of the works of sophistry in art that are popular, does not unconceal any truths or present beauty to the observer, since it has no relationship to the riddle of being a person, since it does not make externally visible the constitution of persons, since it cannot establish what Buber called genuine dialogue, or an I-Thou relation with the observer — because it lacks all these worthy qualities, the most that the producer of the work of sophistry in twentieth-century art can hope for is to generate an emotional or intellectual response among some of the persons who observe the work.

We submit that, at times, a work of fake art may generate an emotional or intellectual response. But, as we show in a later chapter, these emotional responses cannot lead to spirituality, or to a worthy relationship. We all know that intellectual responses can be false or reflect moments of bad faith. And, as Dostoevsky repeatedly showed, quite often emotional responses can deceive and can have no relation to a worthy existence. For instance, in *The Brothers Karamazov*, he shows that an evil egocentric person, Fyodor Karamazov, can be very sentimental, while continuing to act wickedly.[5] Furthermore, emotional responses can be tricky. Marc, in the play, *Art,* was very emotional when he called the canvas totally painted white, that Serge had purchased for two hundred thousand francs: a piece of shit.

Another reason that superficial works of fake art can, at times, seduce their observers is that they supposedly provide entertainment. Hannah Arendt has warned that one of the sad outcomes of what she calls the spread of "mass society" is the devaluing of culture. One common manner of devaluing culture is implicitly, and at times explicitly, to suggest that the sole role of the great cultural heritages, that have been gathered and treasured in the centuries of human history, is to entertain.[6] A recent extreme example of such a cheap devaluing of culture occurred when Walt Disney Studios released a movie in which the Biblical story of Moses is presented as a cartooned movie, similar to their movie *Snow White and the Seven Dwarfs*. The movie about Moses may be entertaining to children, and perhaps to adults who live an infantile mode of existence. But the movie devalues and destroys one of the major stories and spiritual sources of the Judeo-Christian heritage. The movie may be witty and gimmicky, but it is also shallow and vacuous.

Like the Walt Disney movie of the story of the Biblical Moses, probably all of the installations and works of Pop-Art, that are currently exhibited in many museums, seem to have been produced primarily so as to provide entertainment. We believe that almost all of Miro's works of so-called art, including "Woman in a Pretty Hat," are also an attempt to entertain. Many of the producers of the works in this realm of fake art would *not* disagree with the idea that the role of their works is primarily to entertain. According to the historian of art, Herbert Read, the Pop artist, Richard Hamilton, held that Pop-Art should be "Popular, Transient, Expendable, Low-cost, Mass-produced, Young (aimed at youth), Witty, Sexy, Gimmicky, Glamorous, Big Business."[7] This list of the qualities of Pop-Art suggests that these works are primarily an attempt to provide entertainment to the many Philistines that ruin culture.

What do you mean by Philistines? The Random House Dictionary defines a Philistine thus: "a person who is lacking in or smugly indifferent to culture, aesthetic refinement, etc., or is commonplace in ideas and tastes." We therefore emphasize that Hamilton's above-cited list of the qualities of Pop-Art is not only geared toward Philistines. It also suggests that Pop-Art is an ongoing attempt to invade the realm of genuine art with superficial, cheap, slapstick entertainment — in a word, with Philistinism.

Consider Hamilton's statement that Pop-Art is witty. As Plato often showed, for instance, in *Protagoras* and in *Phaedrus*, many sophists have wit. Thus, Plato clearly hinted that a presentation inspired by wit can be an attempt to conceal knowledge, truth, wisdom, and other things that are worthy. Indeed, wit in Plato's dialogues is often coupled with spiritual emptiness, and with the wish to reject truth, and the genuine knowledge that is based on truth.

One of the best contemporary fictional descriptions that we have read of an exquisite wit, which is coupled with spiritual emptiness, and with the devaluing of culture, is found in Proust's *Remembrance of Things Past*, especially in the section titled "The Guermantes Way."[8] Proust repeatedly shows the reader that the renown wit of the Duchess of Guermantes has nothing worthy to offer her so-called friends, except entertainment and, perhaps, social esteem. The Duchess may be bright, clever, and well-read, she may at times exhibit a wry and biting sense of humor. But the witty and glamorous Duchess of Guermantes is also egocentric, she establishes superficial personal relations with all and sundry, including her husband, including her dear friend, Charles Swann. She does not live as a person who endeavors to respond to the challenge of personality, in Bedyaev's sense of the word, and she is quite often downright wicked. The Duchess may be remarkable at entertaining in the social circle constituted of her closed set of peers and admirers, yet, she embraces a superficial way of life. She is steeped in bad faith and cannot relate to beauty or to love or to friendship or to justice.

We concede that the works of some of the sophists whom we reject, say, the works of Joan Miro, Andy Warhol, Jasper Johns, Roy Lichtenstein, Frank Stella, and Richard Hamilton, may be expressions of wit. In addition, their works may, at times be successful gimmicks, or appeal to youth; they may seem glamorous. We would also agree that their superficial and non-spiritual works may shock or entertain some observers. But, we firmly hold that their so-called works of art are very superficial and constitute a devaluing of our culture.

Consider, for instance, Andy Warhol's work that is titled "Marilyn Monroe's Lips." On each of two silk panels, one in pink and one in light blue, using acrylic and pencil, Warhol painted a matrice that is made up of 84 small drawings of Marilyn Monroe's lips.[9] Only the lips are painted. Each matrice is 12 drawings of lips high and seven drawings of lips wide. He mounted the two panels on which there are, together, 168 small drawings of Marilyn Monroe's lips, on a canvas, and he called it a work of art.

Someone may suggest that Warhol has presented a gimmick or produced a work that is witty and gimmicky. Furthermore, one may argue, by exhibiting his witty gimmicky canvas, Warhol can be compared to Marcel Duchamp who sent a urinal, signed by him under an assumed name, to be exhibited in the Exhibition of Independent Painters, which took place in New York in 1917. (The urinal was rejected and not exhibited.)

Our response is that the comparison with Duchamp is very stretched, and basically wrong. Duchamp was honest. He knew that the urinal was an urinal was an urinal. Again, we learn from Gertrude Stein's statement: a rose is a rose is a rose. Duchamp sent the signed urinal to the exhibition's judges because he wanted to express his anger and disgust at the deceit that, he believed, prevailed in the academic cliques that ruled the realm of art. He thus grasped himself and his deed as instituting a rebellion against the mendacity, the bad faith, and the sterility in the milieu of art and art criticism, to which he belonged.[10]

In contrast to Duchamp, Warhol is presenting his work of wit, or better, to borrow some terms from Richard Hamilton, his "popular, low cost, glamorous, young, mass-produced, sexy, witty, gimmicky," canvas, "Marilyn Monroe's Lips," as genuine art. Warhol is thus clearly suggesting that his presenting a work, that is the epitome of superficiality and a gimmick, and holding that it is a work of art is a worthy undertaking. The truth of the matter is that Warhol's canvas is, at best, superficial entertainment.

By these acts, Warhol is living in bad faith; however, his mode of existence is not our current concern. What is significant is that Warhol's popular, witty, sexy gimmicky, and anti-spiritual works are an attempt to devalue our culture, and to efface our heritage of great art.

We believe that the famous, and rather notorious painter, Francis Bacon, produced many genuine and beautiful works of art. We have also found that many of his moving, and, at times, shocking paintings unconceal truths about the Being of beings and relate to the personality of the observer. Applauding Bacon's paintings, however, is not what concerns us at present. Instead, we want to listen to Bacon's response to a question about his relationship to one of the prevailing trends in contemporary art, Pop-Art. The question was asked by Michel Archimbaud, and his conversation with Bacon took place in late 1991. Here is what Bacon told Archimbaud about Pop-Art.

> There's an exhibition of pop art at the Royal Academy at the moment. I went telling myself, "There might be something that can help me. I will get something out of it, or perhaps it'll give me a shock." But when you see all those pictures collected together, you don't see anything. I find that there's nothing in it, it's empty, completely empty.[11]

We fully agree with Bacon's assessment of the collected works of Pop Art. Like Warhol's 168 drawings of Marilyn Monroe's lips mounted on two silk panels, they are all "empty, completely empty." There is nothing to them or in them. Works that are empty, that are vacuous, convey to their observers an attitude of indifference to the world. They create an atmosphere of superficiality, sterility, and impotence. Here we want to emphasize an additional thought, to which Bacon hints in the above citation. These works are fake art because they cannot and will never enrich the observer's existence. Such an enriching of the observer's existence cannot occur when he or she face a work that is empty, a nothing, a bastion of superficiality — as are the works of Pop-Art.

Why have these empty works of art, these bastions of superficiality — be they Minimalist Art, Pop-Art, installations, or other accepted trends that constitute much of the sophistry in twentieth-century art — why have these works succeeded in capturing such a prominent place in almost all galleries and museums that exhibit contemporary art? Why have large amounts of private and public funds been spent to purchase and to house these many works of fake art in public museums?

We attempt to answer these questions, albeit partially, in the next chapter. In order to provide a thoughtful answer, we shall return to the ontology of Berdyaev, especially to the implications of his distinction between master, slave, and free person.

Yet, before we turn to Berdyaev's thinking, it is probably wise to end this short chapter on the widespread superficiality in twentieth-century art by listening again to some of Bacon's thoughts, as expressed in another of his conversations with Michel Archimbaud. Bacon's thoughts strengthen our statements concerning the superficiality of Minimalism and of abstract art; they also add depth to our condemnation of the modules of Carl Andre, as presented in Chapter Two. The following citation also hints that Bacon, at least partially, experienced what Heidegger called the tension between World and Earth in the work of art. Here are Bacon's statements.

> Yes, abstract art seems to me an easy solution. Painting materials are in themselves abstract, but painting isn't only the material, it's the result of a sort of conflict between the material and the subject. There's a kind of tension there, and I feel that abstract painters eliminate one of the two sides of the conflict right from the start: the material alone dictates its forms and its rules. I think that that is a simplification. I also find that the human figure with its constant changes is very important. Abstraction has never been enough for me; it has never satisfied me. It seems to me that abstraction basically reduces painting to something purely decorative.[12]

Eight

MASTER, SLAVE, FREE PERSON, AND ART

In many of his writings, Berdyaev repeatedly points out that persons crave for freedom. Quite often people will fight courageously to attain freedom. Yet, he frequently adds, this craving for freedom only partially discloses the ontology of a human being. Because, Berdyaev explains, "Man seeks freedom. There is in him an immense drive toward freedom, and yet not only does he easily fall into slavery, but he even loves slavery."[1]

Consequently, the ontology of human existence must always take into account the fact that many human beings love slavery, and frequently, choose to be slaves. Hence, those persons, like Berdyaev, who wish to change the world for the better must daily struggle against the widespread human love for slavery, and also against the ontological structures, the political regimes, and the social institutions that encourage and support this love for slavery.

According to Berdyaev, there are three structures of consciousness. He denotes these structures: "master," "slave," and "free man."[2] In this book, we shall use the term free person instead of "free man." Master and slave are structures of consciousness that are always linked to each other, and are quite similar. Both the master and the slave need each other in order to exist as master and as slave. There is no slave without a master and *vice versa*. In contrast, a free person has his or her own qualities, inner life, mode of existence, and individual unique free structure of consciousness. Unlike the master or the slave, the free person has no need of another person to derive and to establish his or her being and structure of consciousness.

We submit that Berdyaev's sharp ontological distinction between the three structures of consciousness is somewhat dogmatic, and most probably influenced by Hegel. We believe that there may be variations of the three structures of consciousness that he describes, and, perhaps, also additional structures. Furthermore, many a person's consciousness may, at times, flow from structure to structure. Berdyaev's distinction seems to be a crystallization of a flowing situation, and it partially limits the complexity of human existence. Despite these reservations, we believe that Berdyaev's dogmatic distinction also presents human existence, and our relationship to art, from an enlightening perspective. Unfortunately, quite often this perspective has been overlooked. In this chapter, therefore, we shall adhere to Berdyaev's distinctions and endeavor to learn from their enlightening perspective.

Without going further, it is evident that a great work of art appeals to the consciousness of a free person. The genuine work of art does not appeal to the consciousness of both the slave and the master because theirs are alienated structures of consciousness, which have stiffled the human longing for justice, for truth, and for beauty. The master and the slave have no relationship to the human quest for spirituality, and will find it difficult to relate to great works of art.

A major argument that Berdyaev proffers to explain why the master and the slave are alienated from human spirituality is that in their structure of consciousness everything is exteriorized, that is, generalized, objectified, rationalized, made abstract. Put differently, in the consciousness of both the master and the slave, there is no inwardness, and no attempt to relate to the mystery of personality or to other mysteries that emerge in human existence. Love is one such mystery that disappears when we attempt to exteriorize it or rationalize it.

Consequently, for anyone who appeals to or relates to the master or to the slave, be it politician, merchant, artist, or sophist, there is no need to relate to the master's or the slave's inwardness. A major result of this situation, whereby a constant concentration on exteriorization and objectivization occurs in the consciousness of the master and the slave, is that in their consciousness the mystery of being a person who responds to the challenge of personality vanishes. This mystery and all other mysteries linked to human existence are smothered under a coating of rather bland objectifications, abstractions, and rationalizations.

An interesting corollary arises to Berdyaev's statement on the link between the lack of spirituality and the trend toward exteriorization, objectification, and rationalization. When a science, say the social science of economics, relates only to exterior aspects of human existence, say, when it views live persons primarily, or only, as rational producers of goods and as rational or irrational consumers of goods, it relates only to the master-slave structure of consciousness. The result is evident. By definition of its realm of inquiry, which is confined to the exterior rational explanation of one aspect of human existence, the so-called science of economics has nothing to contribute to the human craving and quest for spirituality. It is not a science which relates to or explains something about the free person.

The same, however, may be said about the writings of many twentieth-century historians of art, and also about many art critics and quite a few philosophers of art. If the philosopher and historian of art, and the art critic, grasp their role as primarily relating to the exterior aspects of the so-called work of art, if they discuss a work of art, abstractly and rationally, objectifying it without relating to its, say, beauty, which is something spiritual, they are writing their essays or critiques for masters and for slaves. And, because many persons love slavery, shallow art historians, such as Herbert Read, and foolish art critics and philosophers, such as Arthur Danto, are quite popular.

The reason for their popularity is simple. Their writings on art are based on exterior, objectified, rational, and abstract explanations, and their essays persistently smother the mystery of personality and of spirituality. What a feast of exteriorizations and objectifications for the person who loves slavery!

Who has not encountered the devastating outcomes of the smothering of personality and spirituality by the behavior and by the rationalizations of persons who choose to be masters and slaves? Who has not been struck by the banality and insipidity of the accepted trend in the sciences and in the arts of exteriorizing, objectivizing, and rationally presenting everything that has to do with human beings? Only persons who do not struggle for freedom, for personality, for truth, for beauty, for wisdom, for justice, and for spirituality.

Like many other persons who struggle for freedom and for things that are worthy, we have often encountered the smothering of personality and spirituality in the lives of persons whom we met. We have also encountered the smothering of personality and spirituality in the works of social scientists, in the political realm, and, also, in many so-called works of art in museums. This encounter with enslaved persons, who love their slavery, has, for us, confirmed the truths that Berdyaev stated. We learned that he is correct when he suggests that persons who adopt the structure of consciousness of a master or a slave, who are continually engaged in explaining, in organizing, in rationalizing, in objectifying, and in other manners of exteriorizing human existence, — these persons establish situations and relations whereby the mystery of their own unique unrepeatable personality vanishes. Frequently, these enslaved persons also grasp the world as moved solely by external and internal determinations that exclude personality, freedom, and mystery. Consequently, they are quite comfortable with their structure of consciousness, be it of master or of slave.

The twentieth century witnessed extreme situations of wicked political regimes and historical societies in which the master-slave relationship almost totally eradicated freedom, and destroyed the possibility of living as a free person. The evil totalitarian regimes linked to the names Hitler, Stalin, Mao, and Pol Pot were probably the most extreme examples of such master-slave political regimes. But other terrible regimes also ruined freedom and personality, such as the regime in Iraq today under the evil mastery of Saddam Hussein, and the current dictatorship of the wicked generals in Myamar. One result of the extreme situation of totalitarianism was the nurturing of individuals who have no discernable personality, who are boring, insidious, banal, and evil, and quite willing to perform the most wicked deeds. According to Hannah Arendt, an example of such an evil, boring, and banal person, who chose to exist without the quest for personality, was Adolf Eichmann.[3]

We agree that Nazism was a terrible terrifying totalitarian regime. We agree that Adolf Eichmann was an extreme example of banality and evil, since he had much power to do evil, and he daily performed many evil deeds without qualms. With Arendt, we doubt that Eichmann had a conscience. Still, many people are alive today, who live in a democratic or semi-democratic country, and who are not far off from choosing and living a way of life which persistently smothers their own personality and embraces banality. Quite a few of these people have also forfeited their conscience. The extreme example of

Eichmann also throws in bold relief the structure of consciousness of both the master and the slave. Such a structure can only be described as uninspiring, insipid, exteriorized, and yes, boring, banal, and evil. Arendt correctly asserted that such is the structure of consciousness often embraced by bureaucratic, unthinking individuals. Unfortunately, many such individuals thrive in the corporate capitalist regime that currently reigns.

At this point, a pivotal question for our study emerges: Is not a major goal of genuine art to appeal to the free person and firmly to reject the master-slave structure of consciousness? Is not a great work of art a rebellion against the master-slave structure of consciousness and its banality and destruction of personality? We believe that the answer to both questions is: Yes. We believe that this appeal to the free person is also an origin of the work of art.

We emphasize this last point, and, with it the importance of the above question. An alienated and banal person, who chooses the structure of consciousness of master or slave, who constantly lives an exteriorized objectified existence, frequently has forfeited his or her personality. Such a person cannot relate to justice or to beauty or to truth or to wisdom. Such a person will not develop his or her personality, or relate to other persons as personalities. Also, it is dubious that such a person, who is alienated from freedom and from his or her own personality, can establish a worthy relation to a great work of art.

But since many persons do struggle for freedom, since many persons do not at all wish to be slaves, since persons rebel again and again against their enslavement, it is wonderful that there are great works of art that relate to their observers' personalities. These great works of beauty and of truth can inspire people to embrace freedom and to reject the ugliness, the close-mindedness, the banality, the insipidity, the evil, and the deceit that are central to and spread by a master-slave mode of existence. In the twentieth century, totalitarian leaders sensed this point intuitively and rejected all twentieth-century art that inspired freedom. The centuries-old art, that they could not reject, they often tried to coopt and explain that it accorded with their regime's goals.

We can now state a conclusion that arises from Berdyaev's distinctions. The producers of works of sophistry in twentieth-century art, and their many intellectual supporters, are betrayers of our heritage of great art which relates to beauty, to spirituality, and to the mystery of personality. They are betrayers because the works of these sophists can appeal only to the master-slave structure of consciousness.

Only a free person is able and willing to relate to the mystery of personality. Such is probably true in relation to other mysteries central to human existence, such as love. As already indicated, very often the individual who embraces the master or the slave structure of consciousness will not even grasp that major intriguing mysteries exist, mysteries that are central to human existence. Consider what Berdyaev says, in another context, about the mystery of beauty.

> Beauty is the great mystery. One must be initiated into
> the mystery of beauty and without this initiation beauty
> cannot be truly known. To know beauty one must live
> within it. That is why all external definitions of beauty
> are terribly disappointing.[4]

We have grave doubts that any individual who adopts the structure of consciousness of a master or a slave, who exteriorizes all his or her human relations, who continually objectifies and rationalizes human mysteries, who endeavors to explain by exterior relations whatever he or she encounters — we doubt that such an individual will ever seek to be initiated into the mystery of beauty. But in the twentieth century, as Berdyaev often noted, we can witness continual endeavors by many individuals, who are engaged in many walks of life that are prominent in contemporary society, to reject the mysteries of love, of beauty, and of personality.

These people, who persistently reject mystery, include many scientists and other intellectuals, who see their daily calling as the attempt to discover exteriorizations, objectivizations, and rational explanations of reality. They believe that these explanations will eliminate the mysteries that are linked to human existence. These endeavors are frequently coupled with attempts to provide a rational and objective explanation for any hint or any remnant of spiritual existence and of its grace, its mysteries, and its capability to enhance human existence. For instance, some of these people will always find a rational and objective explanation for true love, or for the beauty of Leonardo da Vinci's painting, "Mona Lisa," or for Shakespeare's beautiful poetic language in *Hamlet*. We firmly reject these attempts to reduce the many marvelous mysteries of human existence, such as love or the longing for beauty, or the mystery of great art, or the links between thinking and poetry to certain rationally explained exterior causes or events.

Unfortunately, during the twentieth century, so-called works of art that endeavored to eliminate the mystery of beauty have invaded the public realm of art, and have often triumphed there. This triumph has given legitimacy to many ugly and uninspiring works of sophistry that hang and stand in museums and galleries. Quite often the triumph of non-spirituality has forced us, as observers of art in many museums in the world, to repeatedly encounter grotesque, banal, and bizarre instances of fake art. We state categorically that the master-slave structure of consciousness is promoted by calling these bizarre and grotesque pieces, such "Who's Afraid of Red Yellow and Blue III" by Barnett Newman: works of art.

Learning from Berdyaev, we can now declare that these endeavors to eliminate beauty, by so-called artists such as Barnett Newman, Joan Miro, Roy Lichtenstein, or Carl Andre, appeal to the structure of consciousness of the master and the slave. Moreover, the triumph of sophistry in twentieth-century art encourages both master and slave to retain their enslaved, banal, uninspiring consciousness, and to cherish their enslaved way of life.

Berdyaev's distinction between the structure of consciousness of the master, the slave, and the free person encourages us to pose three questions. Is it not correct that works of sophistry in twentieth-century art — say, Warhol's "Marilyn Monroe's Lips," or Miro's "Woman in a Pretty Hat," which we described in Chapter Seven — have been produced so as to *not* relate to the structure of consciousness of the free person? Is it not true that these many works of fake art *do* appeal to the structure of consciousness of the master and of the slave? Could it not be that this appeal of works of sophistry to the structure of consciousness of the master and of the slave, structures which are widespread, is what makes works of fake art broadly acceptable?

As expected, our answer to each of the three questions is a resounding: Yes! This answer partially responds to the questions that we posed at the end of Chapter Seven, when we asked: Why are superficial works of fake art so popular? Why are large sums of public funds lavished on these works of sophistry? However, we wish to proceed cautiously and to relate directly to the questions that we posed.

Let us now turn straightforwardly to the questions posed at the end of Chapter Seven: Why have works of sophistry in twentieth century art succeeded in capturing a prominent place in almost all galleries and museums that exhibit contemporary art? Why are representatives of the public willing to spend great amounts of money to purchase and to house these works of fake art?

We will now address these question from additional perspectives that are found in Berdyaev's ontology, and are based on what we have explained. Despite this important ontological basis, we acknowledge that the answer we provide is partial. Presenting a full answer would probably require writing another book.

It is not difficult to discover that the princes of contemporary corporate capitalism, and their many lackeys and sycophants, some of whom are writers who address questions of culture, have no relation to the pursuit of justice or to the struggle for spirituality. Nor is it difficult to perceive, as Noam Chomsky's many writings have revealed, that these intellectual promoters of and adherents to corporate capitalism, whose professed cult is the market economy, corporate profit, and financial success, and whose creed stresses production and consumerism, have adopted a mode of existence that embraces the structure of consciousness of the master and the slave.[5] This widespread master-slave consciousness is also evident in the constant exteriorization, objectification, and rationalization of everything that may be even faintly spiritual by the spokespersons of corporate capitalism, be they business men and women, political scientists, journalists, politicians, economists, behavioral scientists, or other so-called intellectuals.

Among the multiple spokespersons who support corporate capitalism you can also list many historians and philosophers who discuss contemporary art and many art critics who write about contemporary art. You should include among these critics the philosopher, Arthur Danto, who, as mentioned in the Introduction, describes non-art as art. Also many journalists who cover contemporary art shows insidiously support the corporate capitalist regime. We firmly believe that, through their acts, all those intellectuals who support sophistry in twentieth-century art are, at least partially, serving the princes of corporate capitalism. From our limited survey of relevant sources written on contemporary art, we have discovered that all of these writers tend to repeatedly present exterior, rational, and objective explanations when they write about those works of twentieth-century sophistry that they believe to be art, say, about Carl Andre's brick walls and red cedar modules.

Herbert Read's very popular book, *A Concise History of Modern Painting*, which we have cited a few times in previous chapters, is but one of many examples of such continual exteriorization and objectivization when writing about works of so-called art. Whichever page you open in this text, you will only encounter exterior objectifying explanations. You will never find a discussion of, or a pointing to, the beauty of a painting. Nor will you find in Read's book any mention of the truth that a painting or a sculpture unconceals. Like Read, all the writers who discuss and justify the widespread sophistry in twentieth-century art by exterior objectifying explanations, do not recognize that by such consistent exteriorization they are disparaging and discarding spirituality.[6] Nor do they recognize that such an exteriorizing approach to works of art supports corporate capitalism.

Since we have cited and attacked statements from Read's book a few times in this study, later in this chapter, we will present an example of such exterior explanations in a book by another writer, Jeremy Lewison. Our major point, however, is that these many intellectuals are dabblers in the realm of art. Since they reject the spiritual dimension of art, their writings are dillentantism. Furthermore, frequently these sophist-dabblers are supported verbally, and financially, by the princes of corporate capitalism. This source of financial support should not surprise us since their approach to art reveals that they embrace and promote the master-slave structure of consciousness. Some of these writers ignore the fact that precisely this degraded, enslaved, banal structure of human consciousness is dear to the princes of corporate capitalism.

Hold it! someone may say. The enslaved consciousness is, after all, not a new phenomenon; it is already mentioned in the Bible, in Exodus 21, in the discussion of the slave who refuses to abandon his master when his period of enslavement has ended. Since that early pre-capitalist period, the enslaved consciousness has been discussed by a host of thinkers; in the nineteenth century Friedrich Nietzsche wrote in many volumes about what he termed the "herd of slaves," and vehemently rejected the enslaved consciousness. You may also include Karl Marx's coining and use of the term, "Lumpenpro-letariat," in the nineteenth century, as another, rather recent, example of a major thinker being aware of and discussing the enslaved consciousness. In short, our history suggests that during the past centuries many ways existed by which a person could have chosen to embrace the structure of consciousness of the master or of the slave. Why do you pick on the twentieth century and on corporate capitalism?

Before responding, we want to agree that the enslaved way of life that corporate capitalism establishes and encourages is merely one of the currently accepted ways by which persons are enslaved, and adopt the structure of consciousness of the master or of the slave. We also wish to mention that Berdyaev often acknowledged that he learned much about human existence from Nietzsche and from Marx.

In this book, we have two reasons for choosing to attack the princes of corporate capitalism, and the capitalist regime, as promoting the enslaved consciousness. First, according to our understanding of recent history, corporate capitalism is the regime that globally dominated the twentieth century; it rose to dominance in the latter half of the twentieth century, and triumphed in the last decade of that century. Indeed, the many discussions of globalization which now, at the beginning of the twenty-first century, are being held in thousands of different forums around the world, are largely a result of the pressure for global expansion of multi-national capitalist corporations.

This trend toward globalization, as Berdyaev noted more than half a century ago, tends to destroy the uniqueness of personality, and the structure of consciousness of the free person. This destruction of personality and of freedom occurs because capitalist-oriented globalization effaces the uniqueness and the difference of persons and communities by its continual attempt to rationalize and to organize everything in accordance with the requirements of what the spokespersons who support this creed call: "the market." In truth, as Chomsky repeatedly has shown, in most cases, the requirements of what is currently called, "the market," are simply the greedy demands for great profits by affluent domineering corporate capitalists. The creed of the market, which is supposedly objective, thus provides the justifications for the rampant exploitation of human beings by the multi-national capitalist corporations, and for the staggering profits that they earn.

Second, because of the tendency in the corporate capitalist regimes to totally exteriorize, objectify, and abstract human existence, because capitalism is essentially and manifestly anti-spiritual and based on greed and exploitation of other human beings, the princes of corporate capitalism seem to have been very happy to verbally and financially support works of sophistry that are also anti-spiritual. Put differently, it is no wonder that these anti-spiritual princes of greed have supported the sophistry that has emerged in twentieth-century art.

As leaders in the political and financial realm, the princes of corporate capitalism also have been happy to pressure political leaders to allocate public funds for purchasing and housing many works of fake art. This political and financial support of fake art, we are confident, has helped the works of sophistry capture a prominent place in art galleries and in museums all over the world. The remarkable film, "Cradle Will Rock," that we already mentioned, is a work of genuine art that unconceals truths which support our statement about the links between corporate capitalism and fake art.

Hence, the fight against sophistry in twentieth-century art is also a struggle against what Henrik Ibsen ironically called: the pillars of society. Today, thanks to their wealth and political power, the princes of corporate capitalism are frequently those who assume the role of the pillars of society. As Ibsen's plays often showed, those persons who are the pillars of society, more often than not, support evil and sophistry. From this situation, whereby sophistry and evil is supported by those who are very wealthy and have much political power, we learn that the fight against sophistry, evil, and deceit has always been difficult, even in the realm of art. Because the fight against sophistry, and its accompanying evils has always been arduous and personally unpleasant, we can now understand why two superb thinkers, such as Socrates and Plato, devoted so much of their time, energy, and thinking, to examining and to rejecting sophistry — including sophistry in art.

Given this harsh contemporary situation, in which evil and sophistry blend, and often triumph, what can those simple people who crave for beauty and for spirituality do? How can we simple people participate in the struggle against sophistry and evil?

Those who choose to struggle against sophistry must acknowledge that they are similar to the Biblical shepherd, David, who went out to accept Goliath's challenge. Indeed, in the ongoing struggle against the evil, the deceit, and the sophistry spread by the sycophantic spokespersons of the gigantic conglomerates that constitute the leadership of today's corporate capitalism, those simple persons who struggle for spirituality and for truth resemble the Biblical David — they have no special arms or armor. Only courage, pluck, and faith in oneself and in the truth can help those who choose to struggle against today's wicked Goliaths.

In parentheses, we add that during the past three decades, we have often been active, together with other persons and groups, in this arduous struggle for truth, for justice, for beauty, for spirituality, and for freedom. Hopefully, this modest book will constitute an additional step in our ongoing struggle for truth, for beauty, and for spirituality. During these years, we have learned that only pluck and personal courage to face gigantic and powerful enemies, together with the insights and the truths disclosed by great thinkers, can help all of us in this strenuous fight against evil and struggle for spirituality, for personality, for truth, and for genuine freedom.[7] Need we add that our enemies have ranged from racists, bigots, and evil politicians, to the princes of corporate capitalism and their many lackeys?

The courage to struggle for truth and spirituality, against the deceit spread by the princes of corporate capitalism and their many sycophants, frequently must emerge in simple daily deeds. Hark again to Berdyaev's understanding of one significant simple step in accepting our difficult task. "But for the liberation of man his spiritual nature must be restored to him; he must be aware of himself as a free and spiritual being."[8]

For those who decide to accept the challenge of personality, we add, that we firmly believe that both relating to genuine and inspiring beautiful works of art, say to the inspiring paintings of Vermeer and Cézanne, and struggling against the widespread sophistry in twentieth-century art, can help a person become aware of his or her personality, freedom, and spiritual nature. This awareness can be a source of inspiration in his or her continual struggle for freedom, personality, and spirituality. In daily life, it can also inspire him or her to seek for beauty.

One immediate undertaking in the ongoing struggle to restore to persons both freedom and spirituality, and to live with the structure of consciousness of a free person, is to uncover the deceit that is spread by many of the supporters of sophistry in contemporary art. At times, these writers endeavor to spread this sophistry under the cloak of respectable scholarly work.

Here is one more example (in addition to those examples we cited in former chapters) of such deceit that appears under the veil of respectable scholarship — we could bring a hundred examples. The example is Jeremy Lewison's book *Interpreting Pollock*.[9] We will briefly indicate that this book is an example of sophistry and an attempt to exteriorize our relationship to beauty and to art.

From the title of Lewison's book, questions arise. Why do the works of a contemporary painter, such as Jackson Pollock, need to be interpreted, instead of being simply looked at, related to, and observed? Or is Lewison's book an attempt to interpret Jackson Pollock, the person?

Lewison does not answer these questions. He flees them into anecdotes about Pollock, the drip-painter, and his works, and into a survey of his paintings and of the exhibits that were dedicated to Pollock's so-called art. Lewison seemingly adds respectability to his writing by using scholarly and, quite often, psychological jargon. In parenthisis we add, that when a so-called scholarly writer begins to use psychological jargon in order to relate to a work of art, or to the show of a specific artist, beware of being hoodwinked!

We will return to the rather perturbing question of the so-called need to interpret modern paintings in a moment; but first, here is one out of many sentences from Lewison's book that reek of exteriorization, superficiality, and deceit:

> Sam Hunter, in his introduction to the touring retrospective [of Pollock's paintings] of 1957-8, referred to the "aggressive spirit of revolt" of the Abstract Expressionists and alluded to Pollock's "bursting masculinity."[10]

We submit that we do not understand the use of the term "bursting masculinity," which Lewison cites favorably, as helping him to interpret Pollock's paintings. Would that term fit any one of the works of genuine art that you may encounter? Never!

"Bursting masculinity" never will fit the musical compositions of Mozart, Bach, or Beethoven. It will also not fit musical works by twentieth century composers such as Igor Stravinsky, Bela Bartok, or George Gershwin. Nor would the term "bursting masculinity" fit the ancient Greek temple, that still stands in a valley in Greece, or Van Gogh's painting of a pair of shoes, works of art which Heidegger described and discussed in his essay on the origin of the work of art. We discussed these works of art in the first three chapters. Nor will the term fit Michelangelo's sculptures, including his non-finished sculptures of slaves that are on display in the Louvre. Those sculptures describe enslaved masculine figures, but definitely not something called "bursting masculinity."

We wonder: How does masculinity burst? Can femininity also burst? Lewison never explains. The term "bursting masculinity" also won't fit the paintings of great twentieth-century artists such as Balthus, Derain, Giaco-metti, Braque, or Alice Neel.

We can now ask: What in the world is "bursting masculinity," and especially where does masculinity burst in a painting? We don't know and never perceived it. And even if we knew what Sam Hunter meant by the term "bursting masculinity," it is an abstract term that has nothing to do with beauty, with spirituality, or with the concrete painting that we may encounter. Moreover, since it is an abstract term, and Pollock's drip-paintings are abstract, how can you identify or point out "bursting masculinity" in one of Pollock's abstract drip-paintings? Our immediate response is: You can't.

Hence, we cannot escape the sad conclusion that these rationalizations of Jeremy Lewison and of Sam Hunter are manners of intellectual masturbation. Put differently, these two shallow writers on art throw these abstract terms at us in order to cover up their inability to convince us that something worthy is to be found in Pollock's paintings. Lewison's and Hunter's formulations are sophistry and deceit.

Let us, however, be a bit modest. We have seen dozens of Pollock's paintings in many museums; we also saw a large retrospective of the paintings of Jackson Pollock, exhibited in the Tate Gallery in London in 1999. In all the instances in which we observed Pollock's paintings, we never perceived something even remotely resembling "bursting masculinity." We did observe that the Pollock retrospective at the Tate Gallery was a large presentation of unbeautiful, unspiritual, abstract paintings that took up many rooms.

Pollock's drip-paintings have no content and no images. Indeed, seeking for "bursting masculinity" in one of Pollock's drip paintings is like trying to identify "bursting masculinity" in one of Andy Warhol's paintings of a can of Campbell's Soup. Therefore, we conclude that the term "bursting masculinity" is empty and is mere sophistry. Using this inane, empty term is an insipid attempt to assign some sort of being to a work of art that does not have that being at all.

The obscurity and sophistry of terms also emerges in Hunter's phrase "aggressive spirit of revolt of Abstract Expressionism," which Lewison also sees as helping him to interpret Pollock's paintings. Lewison seems to have forgotten that paintings that were painted in the style of Abstract Expressionism have, by definition, no content. We repeat: Abstract Expressionist paintings are empty of content — by definition. Consequently, an aggressive spirit of revolt that has no content — that, by definition, is empty — conveys no truth. We should add that, from our experience, an abstract painting, including the paintings of that pioneer of abstraction, Kandinsky, does not convey anything else that is worthy. We believe, and base our belief on the countless times that we have observed such works in museums, that paintings that are termed Abstract Expressionism are unworthy of being called art. We suspect that the painter, Francis Bacon, whose thoughts on abstract paintings were cited at the end of Chapter Seven, would agree with us.

We stress that the paintings that Lewison chose to interpret are works of sophistry. We firmly hold that the endeavor to interpret a painting is already suspicious. Great paintings, such as those by El Greco, Vermeer, or Rembrandt are there to be observed, related to, admired, perhaps even loved. There is no need to interpret them since their beauty shines out and relates to us, the observers. Through this shining beauty, they can inspire our being and our daily life.

Our survey of relevant literature suggests that the interpreting of paintings has only emerged as a scholarly endeavor after thousands of works of twentieth-century sophistry found a place in many galleries and in museums in major art centers. The so-called interpreting of Pollock's paintings is, therefore, merely a manner of spreading and justifying works of sophistry in twentieth-century art under the veil of supposedly respected scholarship. This scholarly sophistry, which includes Lewison's book, is merely a blatant spreading of deceit. But deceit is deceit is deceit, as Gertrude Stein might have said.

In stark contrast to our harsh criticism of *Interpreting Pollock*, the princes of corporate capitalism would be proud of the sycophantic, superficial, abstract, and obscure writing of Jeremy Lewison. They would be happy with his attempt to conceal the vacuity and sophistry in Pollock's paintings, by interpreting these paintings under the banner of legitimate scholarship. The deceit that any thinking person would discover in Lewison's approach would not concern them.

Consequently, whether he acknowledges it or not, by his writing abstract, inane, and unclear phrases, which constitute exterior, objectifying, and abstract explanations, and by his support of works of art that are sophistry, Lewison is also supporting the master-slave structure of consciousness. His writing has nothing to offer the free person who is struggling for personality. At least in a roundabout manner, Lewison is also supporting the dominating corporate capitalist regime, with its structure of consciousness of master and slave, and its many other horrors and evils.

We repeat: Lewison's shallow so-called scholarly book on interpreting the works of fake art produced by Jackson Pollock is supporting the evil and greedy princes of corporate capitalism. Put succinctly, Lewison's book is helping these evil princes in their continual thrust to exteriorize and to objectify everything that is linked to personality and to spirituality. When these seemingly objective and scholarly approaches reign unchallenged, the princes of corporate capitalism can use similar approaches to rationalize away all their own wickedness, and to eliminate all mystery from our lives, including the mystery of beauty and the mystery of personality.

In brief, in his superficial book on Jackson Pollock, Lewison is writing against spirituality, against personal freedom, and against any personal relationship to the paintings.

The firm link between the spread and the acceptance of sophistry in art and the many evils of corporate capitalism accords with Berdyaev's views on social justice. In his book, *The Realm of Spirit and the Realm of Caesar*, he states:

> Social justice cannot be realized without truth and beauty.
> And if, after a social revolution, life is ugly and stands at
> a very low level of the knowledge of truth, this is proof of
> its inner corruption. Ugliness is also falsehood. Beauty,
> as a higher value, is needed for the social reorganization
> of society, otherwise the human type is distorted; style
> and form, image and harmony are wanting.[11]

The citation reveals that Berdyaev would have firmly rejected the many works of sophistry in twentieth-century art that we have been criticizing in this book. His reason for rejecting these works would be simple. The works of sophistry in twentieth-century art are not beautiful, they have no relation to the mystery of beauty, and like Barnett Newman, their producers frequently announced that beauty does not concern them and is not to be sought for or found in their productions.

In addition to rejecting these works of fake art, Berdyaev might also have asked three naive questions: Why in the world should a person strive to produce works that are not beautiful and do not disclose truth? Why would the producer of these non-beautiful works have the chutzpah to call these bland, uninspiring productions works of art? Is it not correct, in the arts, to engage the ability of a person to be creative so as to create works of beauty, works that can relate to and perhaps contribute to the personality of the observer? The answers to these questions are evident.

Berdyaev, knew that ugly persons or ugly situations were often painted by great painters, and that the results were often beautiful paintings. In this context, some of the remarkable paintings of Velázquez come to mind. In contrast to Velázquez's beautiful paintings of ugly persons, the works of sophistry are ugly in themselves. In relation to the works of sophistry in twentieth-century art, we believe that Berdyaev would probably have added that such works of fake and ugly art, that embrace falsehood, testify to the inner corruption of human existence in a world dominated by multi-national corporate capitalism, and by the master-slave structure of consciousness.

We also hold that Berdyaev's thinking reveals an additional grave weakness in the works of fake art that, in other chapters, we have severely criticized and firmly condemned. They have no relationship to social justice. Think again of Jasper Johns's many paintings of targets, maps, and flags, Andy Warhol's "Marilyn Monroe's Lips," Barnett Newman's "Who's Afraid of Red, Yellow, and Blue III," Joan Miro's "Woman in a Pretty Hat," and all the other works that we have shown to be mere sophistry in previous chapters. It will not be difficult for you to grasp that, like thousands of other works of fake art that are found in museums and galleries, not one of these works contributes anything to the human concern with social justice. Nor do these works of sophistry contribute to harmony, to style, and to form. They are barren works, seemingly painted in a spiritual wasteland of human existence. No authentic condemnation of evil and no generosity toward one's fellow human beings or genuine sharing of the Good emanates from these works of sophistry. Indeed, the works of twentieth-century so-called art that we have attacked are mostly ugly; bad faith and falsehood emanate from their Being.

We emphasize: the works of sophistry in twentieth-century art that we have repeatedly criticised have nothing to do with the need to struggle for more justice in our troubled world. The works of fake art produced by Johns, Warhol, Newman, Miro, and all the other producers of works of sophistry are ugly and often repulsive. As such, for a person who longs for beauty and justice, they are no more than uninspiring testimonies of the inner corruption and the ugliness of the corporate capitalist regime that supports them, and of the barrenness of the souls of their producers. But for the many princes of corporate capitalism, who ardently support these so-called artists, and who frequently encourage the spending of public funds on their ugly productions, these works of fake art distract their observers from relating to beauty, and to other things that are worthy. This distraction serves to strengthen the ugliness emanating from the regime of unbridled greed.

Someone may query: It is not common to link beauty to social justice, as Berdyaev does in the above citation. What is the ontological relation which justifies this link?

The answer should not be very difficult for anyone who has followed our brief presentation of Berdyaev's ideas. Almost all of Berdyaev's writings are inspired by his profound concern for freedom and by his personal wish to help human beings live their lives as free, creative, unrepeatable persons. He frequently encourages his readers, as free persons, to struggle for freedom for all human beings, and also, for beauty, for justice, for knowledge, for wisdom, and for all other things that are worthy in themselves. Again and again, he states that only a free creative person, who has struggled to adopt the structure of consciouness of the free person, who engages in living as an unique personality, can attempt to live according to, and to realize, those things that are worthy in themselves, including justice.

Put differently, Berdyaev repeatedly states that only a free person can firmly reject the many lures presented by an enslaving regime and by one's society. Masters and slaves frequently succumb to these destructive lures; hence, they will not struggle for social justice, for beauty, for truth, for knowledge, for wisdom, nor for what Plato called the Good. Thus, works of sophistry in art, works that scorn beauty and truth, that present uninspiring and bizarre abstractions, or cunning gimmicks, or clever ploys, works that are often ugly in themselves — these works of so-called art are lures of enslavement for individuals. They will primarily appeal to masters and to slaves.

From the above citation we learn, however, of an additional dimension to Berdyaev's linking of social justice to beauty. He indicates that you cannot strive for social justice when you embrace falsehoods and ugliness. If you do not seek beauty and truth in your everyday life, if you do not crave for the knowledge that links truths to each other and establishes a deeper understanding of reality and of human existence, if such an approach does not inspire your day-to-day life, your struggle for social justice will be marred and limping. As Berdyaev states categorically in the citation, for social justice even partially to be realized, the free persons who struggle for justice need to persistently pursue truth and knowledge. But they also need to seek for the harmony, the style, and the generosity that works of beauty can convey. Need we add that the greed-inspired way of life determined by corporate capitalism is antithetic to genuine generosity?

We can be blunt in stating our conclusion. The ugly and non-truth-conveying or truth-concealing works of fake art that clutter many museums of contemporary art are a curse to the daily struggle for social justice. They are bizarre and banal works that appeal to an enslaved consciousness and way of life. The fact that they are often purchased and promoted by the princes of multi-national corporate capitalism, and lauded by their many lackeys and supporters only strengthens our statement. These works of sophistry in twentieth-century art have given up on truth, beauty, justice, and wisdom. They encourage the capitalist slave-like way of life, which worships "the market." This degrading way of life consistently sees human beings primarily as objects, not as personalities, and it relates to people as merely avid consumers and rational producers.

Let us repeat. The works of sophistry of so-called twentieth-century art that you find in museums and galleries support the widespread human misery and enslavement that characterizes the corporate capitalist regime that attained dominance in the twentieth century. Vacuous and stupid works of so-called art, such as Newman's painting, "Who's Afraid of Red, Yellow, and Blue III" or Miro's "Woman with a Pretty Hat,"are works of sophistry that do not relate to beauty, to truth, to justice or to anything worthy. Thus they support the master-slave consciousness that is dear to the promoters of the global capitalist regime. Perhaps, these works of sophistry succeed in shocking or in arousing attention. But this success is attained because they appeal to the lowest common denominater in human existence.

Heidegger described the lowest common denominator of human existence, to which we believe the producers of works of sophistry in twentieth-century art appeal, as being dominated by inauthenticity, by curiosity, by idle talk, and by ambiguity. Kierkegaard called this lowly unworthy mode of existence, the realm of the interesting. Lo and behold, frequently, the term "interesting" is used by sophist writers to describe the works of sophistry in twentieth-century art that, repeatedly, we have condemned and rejected.

Hence, before presenting a summary of this book, we shall look at this term — "the interesting." Is there any justification in using this term to present, to describe, or to justify the many works of sophistry in twentieth-century art?

Nine

ART AS INTERESTING

"How interesting!" is a response that you will hear, here and there in museums and art galleries, exclaimed, mumbled, or murmured by the observers of the many works of sophistry of twentieth-century art, including those works of sophistry that we have mentioned and condemned in this book. At times, the response is more abbreviated, and you may here just one word, followed by a pause, or a clearing of the throat: "Interesting... Hmm."

What do these people mean when they use the word "interesting" to describe their response to a so-called work of art? We believe that in most cases they do not mean anything. The reason is that the word "interesting," as quite a few philosophers have noted, describes and defines nothing. Anything can be interesting. Think about it for a minute: from the grotesque to the sublime, from the ridiculous to the hideous, from the banal to the provocative, from the piquant to the bizarre, from the repulsive to the beautiful, from the inane to the wise — anything that fits these and many additional realms to which persons relate can be termed "interesting."

Martin Heidegger firmly rejected the use of the term "interesting" to describe anything worthy; he was especially concerned with thinking. Consider his rejection of the term.

> Interest,... means to be among and in the midst of things, or to be at the center of a thing and to stay with it. But today's interest accepts as valid only what is interesting. And interesting is the sort of that can freely be regarded as indifferent the next moment and be displaced by something else, which then concerns us just as what went before. Many people today take the view that they are doing great honor to something by finding it interesting. The truth is that such an opinion has already relegated the interesting thing to the ranks of what is indifferent and soon boring.[1]

In this citation, Heidegger suggests that using the term "interesting" is a manner of fleeing any commitment to truth and to thinking. It is a manner of veiling one's indifference to what is encountered.

Consequently, when a person announces that a twentieth-century painting or sculpture is "interesting," probably, that person is endeavoring to evade the challenge to question the spiritual worth of the specific painting or sculpture. Questioning, as Sartre pointed out, requires taking a stand; hence, persons evade questioning so as to not be required to take a stand about an issue. They prefer to allow ambiguity to prevail, and the term "interesting" serves them well.

To give just one example, it is quite meaningless for a person to say that Andy Warhol's canvass, "Marilyn Monroe's Lips," described in Chapter Seven, is interesting. As indicated in that chapter, we hold that Warhol's canvas is a gimmick and not a work of art. We suspect that the person who says that this canvas is interesting is using the term in order to evade the challenge to make a definite judgment about whether Warhol's canvas is a work of art or not. If our suspicions prove to be true, such an evasion is a flight from responsibility, an embracing of ambiguity in relation to Warhol's canvas, and a personal adopting of bad faith. It is also a flight from the challenge of personality.

But even if our suspicions are wrong, even if the person who uses the term "interesting" is trying to formulate in language his or her response to "Marilyn Monroe's Lips," he or she has told us nothing about the aesthetic or the artistic or the spiritual value of Warhol's production. Consequently, a person's use of the term "interesting" discloses no truths about the canvas, say, that the canvas is beautiful or ugly, or that it is bizarre or provocative, or that it is teasing or boring. Nor have any truths that Warhol's work might convey been indicated by using the term "interesting."

We do not attribute any spiritual value to "Marilyn Monroe's Lips." We hold it to be a cheap work of sophistry. This lack of spirituality, that immediately meets the observer when he or she encounter the canvas, also leads us to the suspicion that we formulated, whereby persons who call Warhol's canvass "interesting" are attempting to evade reaching a judgment about the canvass. In any event, from the above short discussion we can already conclude that announcing that a work of art is "interesting" is an empty response.

The emptiness of saying that a work of art is "interesting," is revealed, with all its banality, in a work of fiction by the German Nobel Prize for Literature laureate, Heinrich Böll. In his short novel, *End of a Mission*, Böll describes, with much black humor, the banality and the stupidity that emerge in a German courtroom in the small town, Birgler, during the trial of two cabinetmakers — the father, Johann Gruhl, and his son, Georg Gruhl — who together set fire to a German army jeep and played music while it burned. In their defense, the Gruhls asserted that their deed was a work of twentieth-century art; it was a Happening.

In the novel, the Gruhls are firmly supported in their assertion by Professor Buren, who is on the faculty of the Art Academy in a nearby city. In seemingly convincing statements, Professor Buren explains to the court that he is also a sculptor, whose works are relatively well-known. He came especially to the small County Court of Birgler to testify on the behalf of the Gruhls, and to lend academic support to their assertion that burning the German army jeep was a work of art.

When called upon to testify, Professor Buren describes how he understands a Happening as a legitimate work of art. He opens by explaining that, as an artist,

> *he* was not a Happening-man but he had taken a deep interest in and had carefully explored this art which called itself anti-art. It was an attempt, if he understood it correctly... to create a liberating disorder, not form but nonform, nonbeauty in fact; but its direction was determined by the artist, or performer, creating new form out of nonform. In this sense, the incident in question [the burning of the German army jeep] was without the slightest doubt a work of art;...[2]

Böll is ridiculing the idea that anti-art can be art. He is also ridiculing the society which allows its so-called celebrated scholars to declare such an stupid and logically invalid idea. Böll's description of Professor Buren's thoughts is fictional, but this fictional description is based on what frequently happens in the twentieth century in relation to many works of fake art. Note that Professor Buren "had taken a deep interest" in the burning of a German army jeep and other Happenings.

We have given a few examples of celebrated scholars in our non-fictional world who are keenly interested in the fake art that has flourished, and have written books on their area of interest. We have shown that a few of these scholars embrace bizarre and contradictory approaches, which are similar to those expressed by Böll's character, Professor Buren. For instance, we cited in the Introduction a few sentences written by Professor Arthur Danto, in which he asserts that the difference between non-art and art has been "proved invisible."

Böll also shows that such stupid and contradictory ideas can only be supported by empty rhetoric. The vacuity and contradictions in the testimony of Professor Buren are evident; in the same breath he states that a Happening is "not form but nonform" yet the artist was creating "new form out of nonform." Anyone with common sense will grasp that a Happening cannot at the same time be both nonform and new form. But, as Plato repeatedly disclosed, common sense and clear simple thinking never concerned the sophists. What concerned them was to engage in rhetoric that would lead their listeners to accept their arguments, which, they submitted, were not based on truth and on knowledge.

Let us be specific. Professor Buren's testimony is wrought with contradictions, and with obscure language. Yet his testimony arouses the curiosity of the court, and his obscure statements capture the interest of his listeners. His arguments are "interesting," seductive, ambiguous, and seemingly authoritative; as such, they convince lay people, and the judge.

Therefore, he succeeds in helping the Gruhls. Like the sophists whom Plato repeatedly attacked, Professor Buren succeeds in the courtroom, despite and because of his guile, his deceit, and his rhetoric.

In summary, like many supporters of the works of sophistry in twentieth-century art, Professor Buren is using beguiling and contradictory language to conceal the truth about a supposed work of so-called contemporary art. Moreover, he is spreading falsehood and stupidity. It is false, and stupid, to hold that setting fire to a German army jeep, and playing music while it burned, can be a genuine work of art. For the simple reasons that such a deed does not bring into being something beautiful, it discloses no worthy truths, and it has no spiritual value. Nor does this deed relate to the mystery of personality.

Unfortunately, however, we are confident — and Böll's novel intimates that such is the case — that many lay people, writers, and intellectuals would respond to the Gruhls's vacuous and destructive deed with the exclamation: "How interesting!"

"Don't be judgmental!" is another contemporary phrase which you will often hear in intellectual circles. In truth, it is used by many sophists, together with a large proportion of the adherents of various fashionable trends in postmodernism. We believe that they use this phrase in order to conceal their ongoing attempts to eradicate truths and to destroy all spirituality. This eradication and destruction is frequently executed by levelling spirituality down to the lowest possible common denominator, and not judging it.

In addition, we are confident that the phrase, "Don't be judgmental!" accords with the wishes and the demands of the princes of corporate capitalism, who prefer that their many wicked deeds and their ostentatious expressions of wealth not be judged by critics, by thinkers, or by the populace. Here, we will not expand on the many additional reasons this phrase, which demands that we refrain from judging, has become quite popular. We do want to point out that, in relating to art, refraining from being judgmental supports the empty response, "How interesting!"

Whence comes this support?

When I judge something, be it a glass of dry red wine or a painting by Degas, I am relating to the wine, which, say, can be too dry for my palate, or to the painting by Degas, which, say, can be beautiful or uninspiring. In contrast, when I respond to a painting, say, by Jasper Johns or by Clyfford Still with the words "How interesting!" I am not judging the painting. Instead, I am expressing my individual mood or my personal feelings and tastes, and suggesting how the painting may have related to this mood or aroused these feelings and tastes.

This point must be emphasized. When I say "How interesting!" I am not judging the painting by Jasper Johns or by Clyfford Still which I have encountered. At best, I am expressing my own feelings and tastes, or the mood in which I am in, when I encounter the painting. Put succinctly, when I adopt such a non-judgmental approach, what concerns me is not the painting at which I am gazing, but my own individual mood or feelings or tastes. My response to the painting is that of an aesthetic oriented, egocentric individual.

Such an egocentric and beguiling aesthete was poignantly described by Søren Kierkegaard as the narrator A, whom we have mentioned in Chapter Six as narrating the first volume of *Either/Or*.[3] In Kierkegaard's terms, the seductive aesthete responds to a painting, and to everything else that he or she encounters, as a way of playing with one's own moods, feelings, and tastes. The aesthete never responds as a responsible person who is willing to judge what he or she encounters and, perhaps, take action to bring about a change for the better. No, the aesthete is indifferent to everything except his or her moods, feelings, and tastes. To conceal his or her flight from responsibility and from living as a personality, the seductive aesthete views everything as interesting.

Someone may still ask: Why do people evade judgments? Why do the people whom you call sophists repeatedly tell us not to be judgmental?

People evade judgments because, when you judge something, you can be wrong. You take responsibility for your judgment. If I say that Ronald Reagan was a terrible president who did many evil deeds — for instance, he supported the Contras in Nicaragua, and he spread poverty in the United States — when I make such a statement, I may be wrong. But if I say that, as a political or psychological phenomenon, President Reagan was very interesting — when I make such a statement, I will never be wrong. The reason for my never being wrong is that, at best, by that statement about President Reagan I am letting people know my personal impressions; I am not relating to Ronald Reagan as a person who, by becoming president, assumed great political responsibilities. What is more, in the latter statement, by a shifting of the direction of the discussion to my feelings and impressions, they have become important; President Reagan's bizarre, ruinous, and evil deeds have faded into the background.

An additional result of my not being judgmental is also quite immediate. When I merely state that Ronald Reagan is an interesting phenomenon, this statement means that I have decided not to judge President Reagan's evil deeds and ruinous decisions. I have decided not to judge his responsibility, which he did not fulfill, to further justice in the United States and in the world. By this decision, I myself am fleeing from taking a responsible stance.

In relating to works of twentieth-century art, we often have been told not to be judgmental. We reject such shallow approaches. We are willing to be wrong, and to stand corrected. But we refuse to give up our ability and responsibility to judge a work of art. If and when we make mistakes in our judgments, we will duly thank whoever can show us our errors. Our commitment to seeing the work of art that we encounter, to judging it to the best of our abilities, and to supporting beauty and truth is linked to our daily commitment to struggle for justice. This personal commitment to contribute, with our own modest abilities, to establishing a better world, where justice will, at least partially, triumph, requires that we be judgmental every single day. We refuse to relinquish our fidelity to that commitment.

At first, we were quite surprised, while working on this book, to have learned that those individuals who produce and promote works of sophistry in twentieth-century art prefer that we refrain from judging their so-called works of art. In both clear and obscure language, these producers of works of sophistry recommended that we view their works, primarily, as interesting, or as appealing to a mood, taste, or feeling. We rejected this demand intuitively. Later, after studying the writings of Kierkegaard, Heidegger, and Berdyaev, we stated that each work of art should be judged for its beauty, and for its being a work that unconceals truth and relates to the personality of the observer. Only slowly did we learn that the non-judgmental approach promoted by the sophists who support twentieth-century fake art breeds irresponsibility for beauty, for the truth, and for the world that we share with each other.

The reasons that people evade making judgments include a profound component. As intimated, Kierkegaard described this component with flair and depth in *Either/Or*, Volume 1.[4] Kierkegaard repeatedly shows that a person who evades judgement's, and the responsibilities that are always intimately linked to judgements, a person who always seeks to encounter the interesting in life, is dooming himself or herself to live with ambiguities and with seductions. That person will live with very superficial interhuman relations, will be given to moods, will tend to betray so-called friends and loved ones, and will often sink into melancholy. In contrast, by making judgements about truth and falsehood, about good and evil, about the beautiful and the ugly, about wisdom and foolishness, about justice and injustice, we live with spiritual responsibilities. We can relate to persons truthfully and establish worthy interhuman relations such as love and friendship.

Judging is also intimately linked to responding to the challenge of personality. When we take a particular stance on issues, we participate in slowly determining our being, our history, and our future, and in a modest way, the history of the world. For instance, by the taking of a stance that promotes beauty and truth, and encourages persons to respond to the challenge of personality, we also help determine what occurs in that portion of the world to which we belong, and in which our deeds can make a small, but not insignificant difference. Such a taking of a stance is a manner of developing one's own personality.

We will not give more than these few hints about the significance of judging for living wholely, pursuing a worthy mode of existence, and relating to works of art. Yet, we do want to repeat that judging does not occur when a person announces that a work of sophism, say an abstract painting by Clyfford Still, by Piet Mondrian, or by Ben Nicholson is "interesting."

Our final point is that deciding and stating that a painting or a sculpture is interesting usually requires an act of reflection. The statement, "How interesting!" is not a response to a living encounter with the beauty or with the truth that generously flows out to meet you from the great work of art. We have experienced such marvelous living encounters with great works of twentieth-century visual art, recently with works by Bonnard and Monet in two different shows in London. To say "How interesting!", is to refuse to see and to be exposed to this generosity, this beauty, and this truth that emanate from such superb works of art and relate to your personality. Such a response is mediated, it is not spontaneous. Frequently, it is the result of the observer blocking all spontaneity.

But only in a spontaneous, living encounter does a person relate with his or her whole being to a work of art. Hence, stating that a painting or a sculpture is interesting is often a way of evading the possibility of relating spontaneously, with one's whole being, to the great work of art. And a person who rejects relating wholly and spontaneously in one realm of being, say that of art, is frequently ruining his or her possibilities of relating wholly and spontaneously in other realms. Love, which is a relation of the whole being, also may be destroyed by reflection.

In relating to works of art through acts of reflection, the possibility of being surprised and overwhelmed by the beauty of the work of art is frequently eliminated. But many of the writers who support the works of sophistry in twentieth-century art, demand that the observers reflect upon the work and not meet it. Professor Buren's thoughts, cited above from Heinrich Böll's novel, well express this constant promoting of reflection that prevails in almost all writings about the works of fake art. For instance, only by an act of reflection can a person attempt to see a "liberating disorder" in a work of fake art, such as the burning of a German army jeep while one plays music. Or to return to an example from Chapter Eight, only by an act of reflection can a person, perhaps, believe that he or she sees what Jeremy Lewison called "bursting masculinity" in the abstract vacuous drip-paintings produced by Jackson Pollock.

Similar foolish thoughts are often distributed in leaflets near an installation set up in a museum, or near an exhibit in which the observer encounters other works of fake art. We remember receiving such a leaflet in The Kunsthistorische Museum in Zurich before entering a totally empty room, which was painted grey; in the room you could faintly hear a recording of waves breaking on a shore. That so-called work of art was called "Grey Room." The leaflet that was handed to us explained how interesting grey and emptiness can be for us, if we stop to ponder. Forget about the stupidity of this installation. Forget about the sophistry. Our point is that the persons who set up "Grey Room" believed that relating to "Grey Room" demands an act of reflection.

We therefore conclude that the the statement "How interesting!" is a shallow, deceitful way of evading the demand that a person relate wholly and spontaneously to the specific works of art that he or she encounters. It is a statement that wants to seduce us to accept as genuine the many works of fake art that take up many rooms in museums and galleries. To succeed in that role, the statement "How interesting!" is based on ambiguity, and spreads ambiguity.

More than anything else, this statement expresses a flight from the responsibility of the observer of a painting of fake art, or of a person who enters an installation similar to "Grey Room" to question what he or she sees and take a stand. The statement "How interesting!" allows the observer to refrain from stating that there is nothing worthy to encounter when one meets, say, Jacknson Pollock's drip-paintings or the installation, "Grey Room" — no beauty, no truth, nothing. This flight from responsibility of the observer is an egocentric act of cowardice.

Marc's statement, in the play *Art*, that a totally white minimalist painting purchased by Serge is "shit," is courageous, honest, genuine, and unambiguous. It conveys much more truth than the ponderous, reflective, ejaculation, frequently enunciated by cowardly observers of such works: "How interesting!"

Ten

CONCLUSION

As is well known, some of Jacopo Tintoretto's most beautiful paintings are found on the walls and the ceilings of the Scuola Grande of San Rocco (Saint Roch), a building built in the sixteenth century in Venice by the Archbrotherhood of Saint Roch, for its brothers. Tintoretto painted these large beautiful paintings, which depict scenes from the life and death of Jesus, on the walls and the ceilings of all three halls of this large building. He painted the paintings in three stages, from 1564 until 1567 (The Albergo Hall), from 1575 until 1581 (The Upper Hall), and from 1583 until 1587 (The Lower Hall).

One of the most remarkable and moving among these many beautiful paintings is Tintoretto's "The Crucifixion," which takes up an entire wall in the Albergo Hall. In the center of this painting, Jesus is already hanging on the cross, but still alive. One of the persons being crucified with Him is already fastened to the cross, and a group of men are lifting the cross, with the crucified person on it, to put it in its place beside the cross holding Jesus. The third person is being fastened to the third cross, which still lays on the ground. Roman soldiers are beginning to pinion him to it. At the foot of Jesus's cross, Mary has fainted, and a group of supporters of Jesus are tending to her; you can see their horror at what is happening reflected on their faces and in their bodies. Additional officers, soldiers, and horses of the Roman army surround the area, making sure that order will prevail. In the background, the high priest, or, perhaps, another official from the Jewish establishment, which sanctioned the crucifixion of Jesus, is standing, observing the scene.

Two additional men are in the painting. They are situated close to the center of the painting and soon attract the observer's attention. These men are crouched not far from Jesus's cross, seemingly hiding in a large cleft in a wall. They are indifferent to what is happening around them, totally engrossed in their own concerns; they are spending the time shooting dice.

We hold that all the so-called artists, who produced the many thousands of works of sophistry in twentieth-century art, resemble those two men close to the center of Tintoretto's painting, "The Crucifixion," the two men who spend their time shooting dice while the crucifixion of Jesus is taking place.

Whatever the final decisions that historians may make about the twentieth century, they will be unable to overlook the fact that it was crowded with remarkable and wonderful events, yet it also featured many abominable and evil deeds, and no few political crimes of unprecedented wickedness and horror. In a word, it was not a quiet century.

Consider for a moment, and in great brevity, some of the events of this

century in the political realm. This was the century of great statesmen, such as
Mahatma Gandhi, Jawaharlal Nehru, and Nelson Mandela, who taught their
contemporaries, and all of us, that it is possible to struggle for freedom and
justice in the political realm, with nobility and integrity, even in the most
adverse circumstances.

However, this was also the century of totalitarian regimes, which were
based on eradicating the freedom of all human beings and terrorizing and
killing their own citizens and many people of other countries. These
totalitarian regimes featured, among other horrors, the Holocaust that Hitler
ordered and supervised, the Soviet reign of terror and the Gulag Archipelago
which Stalin established and nurtured, and the Cultural Revolution that Mao
initiated and led. These evil leaders, flanked by their cohorts of pernicious
lackeys and wicked supporters, committed some of the most heinous and
abominable crimes against human beings that historians have ever recorded.
Their crimes include the well organized murder of many millions of innocent
people.

Yet, political evil, unfortunately, was not confined to these major
totalitarian regimes. In the twentieth century political colonialism ended, often
to be replaced by harsh economic exploitation of most of the former
colonialized peoples. In addition, from its early beginnings, say, in 1916 in
Turkey, and until the 1990s in Rwanda, the twentieth century also featured
many instances of genocide.

This eventful century also witnessed terrible struggles against racism
and other evils, and for freedom. It was a century in which tiny Cuba
withstood decades of American hostility and economic sanctions, and brought
a more equal society to the Cubans. It was the century when the most
spectacular jewel in the British colonial crown, India, attained independence
from the cruel British colonial rule of two centuries and became the world's
largest democracy. It was the century when the Jews, who had been despised
in Europe and in the world for centuries, returned to their Biblical homeland,
Israel, and established a democratic state there after Hitler's Holocaust which
killed a third of the Jews in the world. It was the century in which the wicked
regime of apartheid and racism ended in South Africa. It was a century in
which many women initiated a courageous rejection of patriarchy and its
degrading evils, and, all around the world, women struggled, fought for, and
attained some freedoms.

And while all these and many other wonderful and horrible events
were occurring, Piet Mondrian and Ben Nicholson isolated themselves, each in
a self built cleft, and crouched there, in that tiny corner of the world, producing
abstract painted works. Nicholson spent his time painting squares of color and
other patterns of colors, while Mondrian was utterly engrossed with painting
straight colored lines and colored blocks on a white and other backgrounds.
We can only conclude that these two painters resemble the two shooters of
dice in Tintoretto's "The Crucifixion." While great events occur before their

eyes, they are concerned with isolating themselves from the events and the call of history and seeking their own bland satisfactions.

They were not alone. Yes, while all the briefly outlined and complex political history, with its limited good and many terrifying evils, was occurring, Roy Lichtenstein was painting his inane enlarged comics strips, Andy Warhol was painting cans of Campbell's Soup or the lips of Marilyn Monroe 168 times, Jasper Johns was spending much time painting targets, American flags and maps, and other meaningless images, Frank Stella was painting his uninspiring and weird "New Madrid" and similar gimmicky weird productions, and Clyfford Still was painting his large and vacuous abstract minimalist pieces. These so-called artists, and thousands of others who, like them, produce works of sophistry, resemble the shooters of dice in Tintoretto's painting.

This point is painful for persons who care about justice and truth and beauty; hence, it is worth repeating. Like Tintoretto's shooters of dice, the many producers of works of sophistry in twentieth-century art flee the pregnant moments of history that they encounter, moments that face them with spiritual demands. They flee these moments into the egocentric, and rather infantile enjoyment that playing around with colors and with abstract, or surreal, or conceptual or popular images can bring. So as not to be alone, and to justify their works of sophistry, many of these producers of fake art, and their no few bizarre supporters in the intellectual milieu, attempt to seduce us to admire their vacuous works. In the process, they are also thus seducing us to join them in their flight from responsibility for our immediate history and for what is occurring in the world.

Hold it! someone may ask. When Paul Cézanne painted apples and other fruits, when Vincent Van Gogh painted landscapes, when Claude Monet painted waterlilies, were they relating to history? Our answer is: Yes!

For one major reason. The paintings of apples and other fruits by Cézanne, the paintings of landscapes by Van Gogh, and the paintings of waterlilies by Monet are beautiful. These paintings unconceal truths, and they relate to the personality of their observers and to the mystery of personality. As such, they are anchored in history, because they relate to the spiritual dimension of human existence. For instance, they show the persons who are observing these works of art that human beings can bring into the world that we share with each other works of beauty. Thus, the apples of Cézanne, the landscapes of Van Gogh, and the waterlilies of Monet add dignity and a spiritual dimension to human existence.

In contrast, the works of fake art that we have rejected have nothing worthy to offer their observers. When they are contemplated, no dignity is added to the being of their observers. At times, these superficial works of sophistry are disregarded and viewed with indifference, sarcasm, or contempt by their observers. There are periods when these works of fake art float like flotsam on the tides of popular moods. But such floating does not make them beautiful or spiritual. Note also that the material that constitutes some of what is called conceptual art, some of the installations, and some of the works of what is called Pop art – the material from which these works of fake art are made frequently resembles flotsam and jetsam.

The great paintings of Cézanne, Van Gogh, and Monet relate to our longing for beauty and for truth, and to our quest for personality and for a creative freedom. In contrast, the sophists who masquerade as artists in the twentieth century produce works that seem to be a mere satisfaction of their own egocentric desires and whims. They themselves repeatedly testified, in bizarre smug writings resembling the essay of Barnett Newman, from which we cited in Chapter Six, that their works have nothing to do with beauty or with the unconcealing of truth.

We have also shown that indifference and shallowness emanate from the works of the sophists in twentieth-century art, and that these works never relate to the personality of the observer. Works of sophistry refuse to relate to the spiritual needs and to the quest for beauty and spirituality of some of those fellow human beings who will observe them. Instead, the works of sophistry appeal to the structure of consciousness of the master and the slave and present us with popular gimmicks or cunning ploys, with seemingly entertaining glamour, and with other clever and beguiling inanities.

We should add that the twentieth century was also a century of great scientific discoveries and a century in which magnificent works of art were created. Albert Einstein is a name that stands alone, at the head of a scientific revolution which includes persons such as Max Planck, Neils Bohr, and Werner Heisenberg. Individually and together, these great scientists added to our understanding of the Einsteinian scientific revolution and of the cosmos in both its manifestations, the subatomic and the cosmic. But there were many other great scientific contributions, and also wonderous technological advances, for instance, the discovery of penicillin in medical research. We shall not attempt to list these great works of scientists who struggled to unconceal truths about the world and the universe that they share with us.

In addition, in the twentieth century magnificent works of art were created by persons who sought to present beauty and to unconceal truths. This politically troubled century featured the poetry of Anna Akhmatova, Rainer Maria Rilke, and Pablo Neruda, the literature of Marcel Proust, James Joyce, and Franz Kafka, the music of Igor Stravinsky, Dmitri Shostokovitch, and George Gershwin, the paintings of Pablo Picasso, Edward Hopper, and Alice Neel — we could go on. While all this glorious human creativity was occurring, Andy Warhol was painting Marilyn Monroe's lips 168 times and mounting the painted lips on one canvas, Jasper Johns was repeatedly painting targets, American flags and maps, and other vacuous paintings, Roy Lichtenstein was painting grotesque enlarged comics strips, and Barnett Newman was painting "Who's Afraid of Red Yellow and Blue III?" — How utterly inane and egocentric!

An important question emerges in the context of Tintoretto's painting. Could it not be that the appearance of all these works of fake art in the twentieth century testifies to a basic lack of courage, the courage needed to seek for beauty, to unconceal truth, and to relate to other persons as personalities? Do not works of fake art also testify to the lack of courage to relate authentically to history, to politics, and to what is occurring in the world?

If the answer to both questions is: Yes!, then it is not surprising that the twentieth-century producers of fake art did not relate to the history of the twentieth century. In a word, we hold that their works of sophistry suggest that these so-called artists were cowards. Consequently, it is not surprising that the producers of works of fake art hid in their self created clefts around the world, playing games with colors and images, and, unfortunately, embracing a mode of existence similar to that of the two men in Tintoretto's "The Crucifixion" who are shooting dice.

Our final verdict on the works of sophistry that have cluttered galleries and museums in the twentieth century can be formulated in five words: *Success does not mean excellence.*

The fact that many of these producers of works of fake art succeeded in capturing headlines in art publications, and, at times, in the mainstream media, or in selling their works of sophistry for millions of dollars to private collectors and to curators at museums where great works of genuine art are on display, the fact that they succeeded in inducing politicians to spend millions of dollars of public funds on acquiring and housing their works — this marketing success does not mean that the producers of fake art produced anything that can be termed excellent. They didn't.

The sophists of ancient Greece also frequently became wealthy, as the successful sophist, Hippias, told the barefoot Socrates in Plato's dialogue on beauty, *Greater Hippias*. These sophists, Hippias added, were also praised and honored in all the Greek cities that they visited in order to teach rhetoric, and to convey and to implement their so-called arts and knowledge. Because he questioned and criticized these successful sophists, Socrates was often scorned, blamed, and ignored by his fellow Athenians. Moreover, the famous sophists in Greece usually completed their lives peacefully, without being put on trial for attempting to teach their fellow Greeks; in contrast, Socrates was charged for his deeds, condemned in court, and put to death in his own city, Athens. But who, today, studies anything that these wealthy, successful, lauded and applauded sophists said or wrote? Perhaps a few historians of ancient Greece.

The successful Greek sophists, like Hippias and Gorgias, are today almost always ignored, while the words of the barefoot Socrates still ring out and can teach all men and women of humankind how to live a worthy life. For one reason. Unlike the sophists, in his daily endeavors, Socrates sought truth, knowledge, and wisdom; he did not crave success. Indeed, Socrates' personal daily quest for the excellence that can be attained by questioning and thinking continues to enlighten us twenty-five hundred years after his death. And his careful inquiries, his well-formulated thoughts, his enhancing ideas, his passion for the truth, and his illuminating arguments continue to inspire us. By these endeavors, and in the way that he coped with his trials and travails, Socrates added dignity to human existence.

Learning from Heidegger, from Berdyaev, from Plato, and from other great thinkers, we have shown in this book that a great work of art is an example of human excellence. As such, it can frequently enlighten its viewers and inspire its observers to strive to live a worthy life, and not to adopt the structure of consciousness of the master or of the slave. Because it is beautiful, because it unconceals truth, because it relates to the freedom and to the personality of the observer, because it encourages persons to be free and responsible, and to strive to create worthy things, great art can engage us and, at times, indicate and suggest to us paths for a good life.

The suggestions on how to live a worthy life that are found in a work of great art, say, to pursue beauty, wisdom, and justice while one continues to seek truth, are quite subtle. At times, we seem to see the suggestions out of the corner of our eye, or we hear them in the background of the beautiful musical piece to which we are listening. Despite their being subtle, these suggestions contribute to the spirituality and to the glory of a work of great art.

In this book, we have attacked the widespread sophistry that emerged in twentieth-century art, because we believe that the pursuit of excellence is central to a worthy human existence. Therefore we have no problem conceding that many works of sophistry that were produced in the twentieth century, and called works of art, have been very successful in the reigning corporate capitalist society. Still, we state categorically that these works of fake art have nothing of excellence to proffer their observers. We have repeatedly shown that these works of sophistry in art are products which should be condemned, ignored, and rejected.

Using Marxist terms, we could add, these works of fake art are a true expression of the egocentricism, the greed, the exploitation and oppression of human beings, the shooting of dice, and the rejection of everything spiritual, including beauty, justice, and wisdom, which are approaches daily embraced by the princes of corporate capitalism, and by their many lackeys and sycophants. The members of this group of supporters of corporate capitalism are the faithful continuers of the bourgeois whom Karl Marx repeatedly attacked.

And it was Karl Marx who forcefully stated that many of the things and ideas produced by the bourgeois — we would add to the list the many works of sophistry in twentieth-century art — should be confined to the dustbins of history.

NOTES

INTRODUCTION

1. Yasmina Reza, *Art*, trans. Christopher Hampton (London: Faber and Faber, 1994), p.3.
2. Martin Heidegger, *The Metaphysical Foundations of Logic*, trans. Michael Heim (Bloomington: Ind: Indiana University Press, 1992), p.12.
3. Harold Rosenberg, *The Tradition of the New* (London: Thames and Hudson, 1962).
4. Arthur C. Danto, *The Visual Arts in Post-Historical Perspective* (New York: Farrar, Strauss, Giroux, 1992), p.5.
5. Jacques Barzun, *The Use and Abuse of Art* (Princeton, N.J.: Princeton University Press, 1975).
6. *Ibid.*, p.84.

CHAPTER ONE

1. Martin Heidegger, "The Origin of the Work of Art," in *Poetry, Language, Thought,* trans. Albert Hofstadter (New York: Harper & Row, 1975).
2. Jean-Paul Sartre, *Selected Prose*, trans. Richard McCleary (Evanston, Ill: Northwestern University Press, 1974), p.156.
3. Robert Bernasconi, "The Greatness of the Work of Art" in *Heidegger in Question: The Art of Existing* (Atlantic Highlands, N.J: Humanities Press, 1993), pp. 99-116.
4. Otto Poggeler, *Martin Heidegger's Path of Thinking*, trans. Daniel Magurshak and Sigmund Barber (Atlantic Highlands, N.J.: Humanities Press, 1987), pp.167-174.
5. Heidegger, "The Origin of the Work of Art," p.25.
6. *Ibid.*
7. *Ibid.*, p. 27.
8. *Ibid.,* pp. 33-34.
9. *Ibid.*, p. 35.
10. Meyer Schapiro, *Theory and Philosophy of Art: Style Artist and Society* (New York: George Braziller, 1994), pp. 135-151.
11. Heidegger, "The Origin of the Work of Art," p.42.
12. *Ibid.*, p.44.
13. Martin Heidegger, *Being and Time*, trans. John Macquarries and Edward Robinson (Oxford: Basil Blackwell, 1962).
14. Tennessee Williams, *A Streetcar Named Desire* (New York: New Directions, 1980).

CHAPTER TWO

1. Herbert Read, *A Concise History of Modern Painting* (London: Thames and Hudson, 1959), p.12.

CHAPTER THREE

1.   Martin Heidegger, "The Origin of the Work of Art," in *Poetry, Language, Thought,* trans. Albert Hofstadter (New York: Harper & Row, 1971), p. 55.
2.   *Ibid.,* p. 54.
3.   *Ibid.,* p. 62.
4.   *Ibid.,* p. 56.
5.   *Ibid.,* p. 57.
6.   Martin Buber, *I and Thou,* trans. Ronald Gregor Smith (New York: Collier Books, 1987). Also, Haim Gordon, *The Heidegger-Buber Controversy: The Status of the I-Thou* (Westport Conn.: Greenwood Press, 2001).

CHAPTER FOUR

1.   Graham Greene, *The Comedians* (London: Penguin Books, 1965), p. 283.
2.   Graham Greene, *The Human Factor* (London: Penguin Books, 1978), p. 38.
3.   See Noam Chomsky, *Necessary Illusions: Thought Control in Democratic Societies* (Boston: South End Press, 1989). Also: Noam Chomsky, *Powers & Prospects: Reflections on Human Nature and the Social Order* (Boston: South End Press, 1996).
4.   Nicolas Berdyaev, *Dream and Reality: An Essay in Autobiography,* trans. Katharine Lampert (New York: Collier Books 1962), p. 94.

CHAPTER FIVE

1.   Douglas Kellog Wood, "Nicolas Alexandrovitch Berdyaev," in: Haim Gordon, *Dictionary of Existentialism* (Westport, Conn.: Greenwood Press, 1999), pp. 41-47.
2.   Nikolai Berdyaev, *Slavery and Freedom,* trans. R.M. French (New York: Charles Scribner's Sons, 1944), p. 20.
3.   Marcel Proust, *Remembrance of Things Past,* trans. C.K. Scott Moncrieff (New York: Random House, 1934).
4.   Friedrich Nietzsche, *Thus Spoke Zarathustra,* trans. R.J. Hollingdale (Harmondsworth, England: Penguin Books, 1961).
5.   Berdyaev, *Slavery and Freedom,* p. 21.
6.   S.A. Blonde, (ed.), *Ensor* (Wommelgem, Belgium: Blonde Artprinting International, 1999), p. 201.
7.   Berdyaev, *Slavery and Freedom,* p. 26.
8.   See: Haim Gordon, *Quicksand: Israel, The Intifada, and the Rise of Political Evil in Democracies* (East Lansing, Mich.: Michigan State University Press, 1995), chs. 2-4.
9.   Berdyaev, *Slavery and Freedom,* p. 27.
10. Patricia Hills, *Alice Neel* (New York: Harry N. Abrams, 1983), p. 108.

CHAPTER SIX

1. Nicolas Berdyaev, *Slavery and Freedom*, trans. R. M. French (New York: Charles Scribner's Sons, 1944), p. 42.
2. Søren Kierkegaard, *Either/Or,* Volume 1, trans. David F. Swenson and Lillian Marvin Swenson (Princeton: Princeton University Press, 1959), p. 28.
3. Herbert Read, *A Concise History of Modern Painting* (London: Thames and Hudson, 1974), p. 293.
4. *Ibid.*, pp. 292-293.
5. Barnett Newman "The Sublime Is Now," in Herschel B. Chipp (ed.), *Theories of Modern Art* (Berkeley, Cal.: University of California Press, 1968), p. 552.
6. *Ibid.*, p. 553.
7. *Ibid.*

CHAPTER SEVEN

1. Marcel Proust, *Rememberance of Things Past*, Vol. 2. trans. C.K. Scott Moncrieff (New York: Random House, 1934), p.559.
2. Herbert Read, *A Concise History of Modern Painting* (London: Thames and Hudson, 1974), p.293.
3. Rosa Maria Maler, *Fundacio Joan Miro Guidebook* (Barcelona: Skira Carrogio, 1999), p.84 & p.89.
4. Martin Buber, *I and Thou*, trans. Ronald Gregor Smith (New York: Collier Books, 1987). Haim Gordon, *Dance, Dialogue, and Despair: Existentialist Philosophy and Education for Peace in Israel* (Tuscaloosa, Ala: University of Alabama Press, 1986.) Also Haim Gordon and Rina Shtelman, "A Buberian Educational Approach to Cubist Art." *The Journal of Aesthetic Education.* 34:1 (Spring 2000), pp. 97-102.
5. Fyodor Dostoevsky. *The Brothers Karamazov*, trans. Richard Pevear and Larissa Volokhonsky (New York: Vintage Books, 1991). See esp. the chapter "The Old Buffoon," pp. 38-46.
6. Hannah Arendt, *Between Past and Future: Eight Exercises in Political Thought* (London: Penguin Books, 1956). See esp. ch. 6, "The Crisis in Culture: Its Social and Political Significance."
7. Read, *A Concise History*, p. 299.
8. Marcel Proust, *Remembrance of Things Past*, Vol. 1, trans C.K. Scott Moncrief (New York: Random House, 1934). See esp. Book 3, "The Guermantes Way."
9. Andy Warhol's "Marylin Monroe's Lips" (1962) is in the Hirshhorn Museum of the Smithsonian Institution, Washington, D.C. A colored photograph can be found in: Tilman Osterworld, *Pop Art* (Koln: Taschen, 1999), p. 13.
10. Robert Motherwell, ed., *The Dada Painters and Poets: An Anthology* (Cambridge, Mass.: Harvard University Press, 1979), p. 139.
11. Francis Bacon*: In Conversation with Michel Archimbaud* (London: Phaidon Press, 1993), p. 45.
12. *Ibid.*, p. 145.

CHAPTER EIGHT

1. Nikolai Berdyaev, *Slavery and Freedom*, trans. R.M. French (New York: Charles Scribner's Sons, 1944), p. 59.
2. *Ibid.*, p. 60.
3. Hannah Arendt, *Eichmann in Jerusalem: A Report on the Banality of Evil* (London: Penguin, 1965).
4. Nicolas Berdyaev, *The Meaning of the Creative Act*, trans. Donald A. Lowrie (London: Victor Gollancz, 1955), p. 246.
5. Noam Chomsky, *Deterring Democracy* (London: Verso, 1991). Also: *Powers and Prospects: Reflections on Human Nature and the Social Order* (Boston: South End Press, 1996).
6. Herbert Read, *A Concise History of Modern Painting* (London: Thames and Hudson, 1974).
7. See: Haim Gordon and Rivca Gordon, *Sartre and Evil: Guidelines for a Struggle* (Westport, Conn.: Greenwood Press, 1995). Also: Haim Gordon, *Quicksand: Israel, The Intifada, and the Rise of Political Evil in Democracies* (East Lansing, Mich: Michigan State University Press, 1995).
8. Berdyaev, *Slavery and Freedom*, p. 60.
9. Jeremy Lewison, *Interpreting Pollock* (London: Tate Gallery Publishing, 1999).
10. *Ibid*, p. 70.
11. Nicolas Berdyaev, *The Realm of Spirit and the Realm of Caesar*, trans. Donald A. Lowrie (London: Victor Gollancz, 1952), pp. 93-94.

CHAPTER NINE

1. Martin Heidegger, *What Is Called Thinking*, trans J. Glenn Gray and F. Wieck (New York: Harper & Row, 1968), p. 5.
2. Heinrich Böll, *End of a Mission*, trans. Leila Vennewitz (Evanston, Ill.: Northwestern University Press, 1994), p. 174.
3. Søren Kierkegaard, *Either/Or* Volume1. Trans. David F. Swenson and Lillian Marvin Swenson (Princeton: Princeton University Press, 1959).
4. *Ibid.*

BIBLIOGRAPHY

Arendt, Hannah. *Between Past and Future: Eight Exercises in Political Thought.* London: Penguin Books, 1956.

———. *Eichmann in Jerusalem: A Report on the Banality of Evil.* London: Penguin, 1965.

Bacon, Francis. *Bacon Francis: In Conversation with Michel Archimbaud.* London: Phaidon Press, 1993.

Barzun, Jacques. *The Use and Abuse of Art.* Princeton, N.J.: Princeton University Press, 1975.

Berdyaev, Nicolas. *Dream and Reality: An Essay in Autobiography.* Translated by Katharine Lampert. New York: Collier Books 1962.

———. *Slavery and Freedom.* Translated by R.M. French. New York: Charles Scribner's Sons, 1944.

———. *The Meaning of the Creative Act.* Translated by Donald A. Lowrie. London: Victor Gollancz, 1955.

———. *The Realm of Spirit and the Realm of Caesar.* Translated by Donald A. Lowrie, London: Victor Gollancz, 1952.

Bernasconi, Robert. *Heidegger in Question: The Art of Existing.* Atlantic Highlands, N.J.: Humanities Press, 1993.

Blonde, S.A. (ed.), *Ensor.* Wommelgem, Belgium: Blonde Artprinting International, 1999.

Böll, Heinrich. *End of a Mission.* Translated by Leila Vennewitz. Evanston, Ill.: Northwestern University Press, 1994.

Buber, Martin. *I and Thou.* Translated by Ronald Gregor Smith. New York: Collier Books, 1987.

Chipp, Herschel B. (ed.), *Theories of Modern Art.* Berkeley, Cal.: University of California Press, 1968.

Chomsky, Noam. *Necessary Illusions: Thought Control in Democratic Societies.* Boston: South End Press, 1989.

———. *Powers & Prospects: Reflections on Human Nature and the Social Order.* Boston: South End Press, 1996.

————. *Deterring Democracy*. London: Verso, 1991. Also: *Powers and Prospects: Reflections on Human Nature and the Social Order*. Boston: South End Press, 1996.

Danto, Arthur C. *The Visual Arts in Post-Historical Perspective*. New York: Farrar, Strauss, Giroux, 1992.

Dostoevsky, Fyodor. *The Brothers Karamazov*. Translated by Richard Pevear and Larissa Volokhonsky. New York: Vintage Books, 1991.

Gordon, Haim. *The Heidegger-Buber Controversy: The Status of the I-Thou*. Westport Conn.: Greenwood Press, 2001.

————. *Quicksand: Israel, The Intifada, and the Rise of Political Evil in Democracies*. East Lansing, Mich.: Michigan State University Press, 1995.

————. *Dance, Dialogue, and Despair: Existentialist Philosophy and Education for Peace in Israel*. Tuscaloosa, Ala: University of Alabama Press, 1986.

————. *Dictionary of Existentialism*. Westport, Conn: Greenwood Press, 1999.

Gordon, Haim and Rina Shtelman, "A Buberian Educational Approach to Cubist Art." *The Journal of Aesthetic Education*. 34:1 (Spring 2000).

Gordon, Haim and Rivca Gordon. *Sartre and Evil: Guidelines for a Struggle*. Westport, Conn.: Greenwood Press, 1995.

Greene, Graham. *The Comedians*. London: Penguin Books, 1965.

————. *The Human Factor*. London: Penguin Books, 1978.

Heidegger, Martin. *The Metaphysical Foundations of Logic*. Translated by Michael Heim. Bloomington: Ind: Indiana University Press, 1992.

————. *Poetry, Language, Thought*. Translated by Albert Hofstadter. New York: Harper & Row, 1975.

————. *Being and Time*. Translated by John Macquarries and Edward Robinson. Oxford: Basil Blackwell, 1962.

————. *What Is Called Thinking*. Translated by J. Glenn Gray and F. Wieck. New York: Harper & Row, 1968.

Hills, Patricia . *Alice Neel*. New York: Harry N. Abrams, 1983.

Kierkegaard, Søren. *Either/Or*, Volume 1. Translated by David F. Swenson and Lillian Marvin Swenson. Princeton: Princeton University Press, 1959.

Lewison, Jeremy. *Interpreting Pollock*. London: Tate Gallery Publishing, 1999.

Maler, Rosa Maria. *Fundacio Joan Miro Guidebook*. Barcelona: Skira Carrogio, 1999.

Motherwell, Robert. ed.. *The Dada Painters and Poets: An Anthology*. Cambridge, Mass.: Harvard University Press, 1979.

Nietzsche, Friedrich. *Thus Spoke Zarathustra*. Translated by. R.J. Hollingdale, Harmondsworth, England: Penguin Books, 1961.

Osterworld, Tilman. *Pop Art*. Koln: Taschen, 1999.

Plato, *The Collected Dialogues*. ed. Edith Hamilton and Huntington Cairns. Princeton, N.J.: Princeton University Press, 1963

Poggeler, Otto. *Martin Heidegger's Path of Thinking*. Translated by Daniel Magurshak and Sigmund Barber. Atlantic Highlands, N.J.: Humanities Press, 1987.

Proust, Marcel. *Remembrance of Things Past*. Translated by C.K. Scott Moncrieff. New York: Random House, 1927.

Read, Herbert. *A Concise History of Modern Painting*. London: Thames and Hudson, 1959.

Reza, Yasmina. *Art*. Trans. Christopher Hampton. London: Faber and Faber, 1994.

Rosenberg, Harold. *The Tradition of the New*. London: Thames and Hudson, 1962.

Sartre, Jean-Paul. *Selected Prose*. Translated by Richard McCleary. Evanston, Ill: Northwestern University Press, 1974.

Schapiro, Meyer. *Theory and Philosophy of Art: Style, Artist, and Society*. New York: George Braziller, 1994.

Williams, Tennessee. *A Streetcar Named Desire*. New York: New Directions, 1980.

ABOUT THE AUTHORS

Haim Gordon is Professor of Education at Ben Gurion University in Israel. His most recent books are: *Dwelling Poetically: Educational Challenges in Heidegger's Thinking on Poetry* (2000), *The Heidegger-Buber Controversy: The Status of the I-Thou* (2001), *Sartre's Philosophy and the Challenge of Education* (with Rivca Gordon 2001).

Rivca Gordon is Director of the Foundation for Democratic Education in Israel. She has co-authored *Sartre's Philosophy and the Challenge of Education* (2001). Her latest published paper is "The Problem of Joy in Sartre's Ontology."

INDEX

A

Abstract Expressionism, 34, 70, 98
Abstraction, 64
Akhmatova, Anna, 114
Andre, Carl, 24, 32-33, 35, 39-40, 42, 47, 60, 66, 80, 86, 91, 93
Archimbaud, Michel, 85-86
Arendt, Hannah, 83, 89-90
Athens, 42, 115

B

Bach, Johann Sebastian, 97
Bacon, Francis, 1, 28, 85-86, 98
Balthus, (Balthasar Klossowski) 1, 18, 47, 68-70, 99
Barcelona, 81
Bartok, Bela, 99
Barzun, Jacques, 7-8, 13, 56
    The Use and Abuse of Art, 7
Beckman, Max, 50, 70
Beethoven, Ludwig van, 97
Being, 2, 6-7, 23, 25, 28, 31, 41, 44, 49, 53, 59, 79-80
Being of beings, 19, 31, 53, 81, 85
Berdyaev, Nicolas, ix, 1, 5, 8-9, 31, 48, 56, 59-69, 71, 73-78, 82, 84, 86, 87-92, 94, 96-97, 99-101, 108, 116
    Slavery and Freedom, xi, 9, 60
    The Realm of Spirit and the Realm of Ceasar, 99
Berlin, 59
Bernasconi, Robert, 14
Bible, 37-38, 93
Bohr, Niels, 7, 114
Böll, Heinrich, 104-106, 109
    End of a Mission, 104
Bonnard, Pierre, 1, 109
Botticelli, Sandro, 35
Braque, Georges, 1, 97
British Museum, 20
Brussels, 64-65
Buber, Martin, 5, 8, 46, 82-83

C

Cairo, 20, 43
Cairo Museum, 21
Canaletto, (Giovani Antonio Canal) 51-52, 55
capitalism, 10, 56, 92-95, 98, 101
Cézanne, Paul, 41, 61, 79, 96, 113-114
Chagall, Marc, 1
Chardin, Jean, 44
Cheops Pyramid, 21, 22
China, 66
Chomsky, Noam, 55, 92, 94
Conceptualists, 2
Contras, 107
"Cradle Will Rock," 55, 94
Cuba, 112

D

Dada, 64, 70
Danto, Arthur C., 6-7, 56, 93
    The Visual Arts in Post-Historical Perspective, 6
Degas, Hilaire Germain Edgar, 106
Derain, André, 70, 97
Descartes, René, 15
    Meditation on First Philosophy, 15
Dix, Otto, 1, 50
Dostoevsky, Fyodor Mikhailovich, 38, 83
    The Brothers Karamazov, 38, 83
Dubuffet, Jean, 22
Duchamp, Marcel, 2, 44, 85

E

Egypt, 20, 21, 22, 43
Eichmann, Adolf, 89
Einstein, Albert, 7, 114
El Greco, (Dominico Theotocopuli), 98
Ensor, James, 64-66, 70, 78
Europe, 112
Expressionism, 98

F

Far East, 66
fascism, 49, 50
Faulkner, William, 26
First Samuel, 38
Florence, 37
France, 7
Franco, Francisco, 74
Freud, Lucian, 1,
Frost, Robert, 26

G

Gandhi, Mohandas, 112
Georges Pompidou Center for Culture
   and Modern Art, 22
Germany, 49
Gershwin, George, 26-27, 37, 39, 97,
   114
      Porgy and Bess, 27
      Rhaphsody in Blue, 27
Giacometti, Alberto, 97
Giza pyramids, 20-21, 43
Great Pyramid, 21, 22
Greece, 97, 115
Greene, Graham, 49, 53, 55
      The Comedians, 49
      The Human Factor, 53
Guardi, Francesco, 51, 52, 55
Gulag Archipelago, 112

H

Hamilton, Richard, 83-85
Hegel, Georg Friedrich Wilhelm, 3, 8,
   14, 35, 87
Heidegger, Martin, ix, 1-3, 5, 7-8, 13-
   28, 33, 35, 37-48, 50, 52-53, 56, 60,
   65, 79, 82, 97, 102-103, 108, 116
      Being and Time, 7, 23, 25, 31
      "The Origin of the Work of Art,"
         ix, 8, 13-14, 31, 37, 43
Heisenberg, Werner, 7, 114
Hills, Patricia, 70
Hitler, Adolf, 74, 89, 112
Holocaust, 13, 112

Hopper, Edward, 1, 5, 14, 26, 39-43,
   45 ,47 ,53 ,82 ,114
      "Nighthawks," 5, 14, 39, 43-45, 82
Hunter, Sam, 97-98
Hussein, Saddam, 89
Husserl, Edmund, 60

I

Ibsen, Henrik, 95
India, 112
Installationists, 2
Iraq, 89
Israel, 38, 112
Italy, 37

J

jazz, 27
Johns, Jasper, 2, 5, 18, 29, 39-40, 42,
   49, 53, 56, 60, 66, 71, 80, 84, 100,
   106, 113
Joyce, James, 114

K

Kafka, Franz, 114
Kandinsky, Vasili, 18, 29, 69, 98
Kant, Immanuel, 8
Kepler, Johann, 45
Kierkegaard, Søren, 9, 60, 74-77, 102,
   107-108
      Either/Or, , 74-75, 107-109
Kiev, 59
Kunsthistorische Museum, 109

L

Leibniz, Gottfried Wilhelm, 62
Lewison, Jeremy, 93, 96-99, 109
      Interpreting Pollock, 96, 98
Lichtenstein, Roy, 2, 25-26, 41-42, 49,
   60, 66, 71, 80, 84, 91, 113-115
London, 20
Louvre, 97

VIBS

The **Value Inquiry Book Series** is co-sponsored by:

Adler School of Professional Psychology
American Indian Philosophy Association
American Maritain Association
American Society for Value Inquiry
Association for Process Philosophy of Education
Canadian Society for Philosophical Practice
Center for Bioethics, University of Turku
Center for International Partnerships, Rochester Institute of Technology
Center for Professional and Applied Ethics, University of North Carolina at
Charlotte
Center for Research in Cognitive Science, Autonomous University of
Barcelona
Centre for Applied Ethics, Hong Kong Baptist University
Centre for Cultural Research, Aarhus University
Centre for Professional Ethics, University of Central Lancashire
Centre for the Study of Philosophy and Religion, College of Cape Breton
College of Education and Allied Professions, Bowling Green State University
Concerned Philosophers for Peace
Conference of Philosophical Societies
Department of Moral and Social Philosophy, University of Helsinki
Gannon University
Gilson Society
Ikeda University
Institute of Philosophy of the High Council of Scientific Research, Spain
International Academy of Philosophy of the Principality of Liechtenstein
International Center for the Arts, Humanities, and Value Inquiry
International Society for Universal Dialogue

Natural Law Society
Personalist Discussion Group
Philosophical Society of Finland
Philosophy Born of Struggle Association
Philosophy Seminar, University of Mainz
Pragmatism Archive
R.S. Hartman Institute for Formal and Applied Axiology
Research Institute, Lakeridge Health Corporation
Russian Philosophical Society
Society for Iberian and Latin-American Thought
Society for the Philosophic Study of Genocide and the Holocaust
Society for the Philosophy of Sex and Love
Yves R. Simon Institute.

Titles Published

1.   Noel Balzer, *The Human Being as a Logical Thinker.*

2.   Archie J. Bahm, *Axiology: The Science of Values.*

3.   H. P. P. (Hennie) Lötter, *Justice for an Unjust Society.*

4.   H. G. Callaway, *Context for Meaning and Analysis: A Critical Study in the Philosophy of Language.*

5.   Benjamin S. Llamzon, *A Humane Case for Moral Intuition.*

6.   James R. Watson, *Between Auschwitz and Tradition: Postmodern Reflections on the Task of Thinking.* A volume in **Holocaust and Genocide Studies.**

7.   Robert S. Hartman, *Freedom to Live: The Robert Hartman Story,* edited by Arthur R. Ellis.   A volume in **Hartman Institute Axiology Studies.**

8.   Archie J. Bahm, *Ethics: The Science of Oughtness.*

9.   George David Miller, *An Idiosyncratic Ethics; Or, the Lauramachean Ethics.*

10. Joseph P. DeMarco, *A Coherence Theory in Ethics.*

11. Frank G. Forrest, *Valuemetrics^N: The Science of Personal and Professional Ethics.* A volume in **Hartman Institute Axiology Studies.**

12. William Gerber, *The Meaning of Life: Insights of the World's Great Thinkers.*

13. Richard 'I. Hull, Editor, *A Quarter Century of Value Inquiry: Presidential Addresses of the American Society for Value Inquiry.* A volume in **Histories and Addresses of Philosophical Societies.**

14. William Gerber, *Nuggets of Wisdom from Great Jewish Thinkers: From Biblical Times to the Present.*

15. Sidney Axinn, *The Logic of Hope: Extensions of Kant's View of Religion.*

16. Messay Kebede, *Meaning and Development.*

17. Amihud Gilead, *The Platonic Odyssey: A Philosophical-Literary Inquiry into the* Phaedo.

18. Necip Fikri Alican, *Mill's Principle of Utility: A Defense of John Stuart Mill's Notorious Proof.* A volume in **Universal Justice.**

19. Michael H. Mitias, Editor, *Philosophy and Architecture.*

20. Roger T. Simonds, *Rational Individualism: The Perennial Philosophy of Legal Interpretation.* A volume in **Natural Law Studies.**

21. William Pencak, *The Conflict of Law and Justice in the Icelandic Sagas.*

22. Samuel M. Natale and Brian M. Rothschild, Editors, *Values, Work, Education: The Meanings of Work.*

23. N. Georgopoulos and Michael Heim, Editors, *Being Human in the Ultimate: Studies in the Thought of John M. Anderson.*

24. Robert Wesson and Patricia A. Williams, Editors, *Evolution and Human Values.*

25. Wim J. van der Steen, *Facts, Values, and Methodology: A New Approach to Ethics.*

40. Samantha Brennan, Tracy Isaacs, and Michael Milde, Editors, *A Question of Values: New Canadian Perspectives in Ethics and Political Philosophy.*

41. Peter A. Redpath, *Cartesian Nightmare: An Introduction to Transcendental Sophistry.* A volume in **Studies in the History of Western Philosophy.**

42. Clark Butler, *History as the Story of Freedom: Philosophy in Intercultural Context,* with Responses by sixteen scholars.

43. Dennis Rohatyn, *Philosophy History Sophistry.*

44. Leon Shaskolsky Sheleff, *Social Cohesion and Legal Coercion: A Critique of Weber, Durkheim, and Marx.* Afterword by Virginia Black.

45. Alan Soble, Editor, *Sex, Love, and Friendship: Studies of the Society for the Philosophy of Sex and Love, 1977-1992.* A volume in **Histories and Addresses of Philosophical Societies.**

46. Peter A. Redpath, *Wisdom's Odyssey: From Philosophy to Transcendental Sophistry.* A volume in **Studies in the History of Western Philosophy.**

47. Albert A. Anderson, *Universal Justice: A Dialectical Approach.* A volume in **Universal Justice.**

48. Pio Colonnello, *The Philosophy of José Gaos.* Translated from Italian by Peter Cocozzella. Edited by Myra Moss. Introduction by Giovanni Gullace. A volume in **Values in Italian Philosophy.**

49. Laura Duhan Kaplan and Laurence F. Bove, Editors, *Philosophical Perspectives on Power and Domination: Theories and Practices.* A volume in **Philosophy of Peace.**

50. Gregory F. Mellema, *Collective Responsibility.*

51. Josef Seifert, *What Is Life? The Originality, Irreducibility, and Value of Life.* A volume in **Central-European Value Studies.**

52. William Gerber, *Anatomy of What We Value Most.*

53. Armando Molina, *Our Ways: Values and Character,* edited by Rem B. Edwards. A volume in **Hartman Institute Axiology Studies.**

54. Kathleen J. Wininger, *Nietzsche's Reclamation of Philosophy.* A volume in **Central-European Value Studies.**

55. Thomas Magnell, Editor, *Explorations of Value.*

56. HPP (Hennie) Lötter, *Injustice, Violence, and Peace: The Case of South Africa.* A volume in **Philosophy of Peace.**

57. Lennart Nordenfelt, *Talking About Health: A Philosophical Dialogue.* A volume in **Nordic Value Studies.**

58. Jon Mills and Janusz A. Polanowski, *The Ontology of Prejudice.* A volume in **Philosophy and Psychology.**

59. Leena Vilkka, *The Intrinsic Value of Nature.*

60. Palmer Talbutt, Jr., *Rough Dialectics: Sorokin's Philosophy of Value,* with Contributions by Lawrence T. Nichols and Pitirim A. Sorokin.

61. C. L. Sheng, *A Utilitarian General Theory of Value.*

62. George David Miller, *Negotiating Toward Truth: The Extinction of Teachers and Students.* Epilogue by Mark Roelof Eleveld. A volume in **Philosophy of Education.**

63. William Gerber, *Love, Poetry, and Immortality: Luminous Insights of the World's Great Thinkers.*

64. Dane R. Gordon, Editor, *Philosophy in Post-Communist Europe.* A volume in **Post-Communist European Thought.**

65. Dane R. Gordon and Józef Niznik, Editors, *Criticism and Defense of Rationality in Contemporary Philosophy.* A volume in **Post-Communist European Thought.**

66. John R. Shook, *Pragmatism: An Annotated Bibliography, 1898-1940.* With Contributions by E. Paul Colella, Lesley Friedman, Frank X. Ryan, and Ignas K. Skrupskelis.

67. Lansana Keita, *The Human Project and the Temptations of Science.*

68. Michael M. Kazanjian, *Phenomenology and Education: Cosmology, Co-Being, and Core Curriculum.* A volume in **Philosophy of Education.**

69. James W. Vice, *The Reopening of the American Mind: On Skepticism and Constitutionalism.*

70. Sarah Bishop Merrill, *Defining Personhood: Toward the Ethics of Quality in Clinical Care.*

71. Dane R. Gordon, *Philosophy and Vision.*

72. Alan Milchman and Alan Rosenberg, Editors, *Postmodernism and the Holocaust.* A volume in **Holocaust and Genocide Studies.**

73. Peter A. Redpath, *Masquerade of the Dream Walkers: Prophetic Theology from the Cartesians to Hegel.* A volume in **Studies in the History of Western Philosophy.**

74. Malcolm D. Evans, *Whitehead and Philosophy of Education: The Seamless Coat of Learning.* A volume in **Philosophy of Education.**

75. Warren E. Steinkraus, *Taking Religious Claims Seriously: A Philosophy of Religion,* edited by Michael H. Mitias. A volume in **Universal Justice.**

76. Thomas Magnell, Editor, *Values and Education.*

77. Kenneth A. Bryson, *Persons and Immortality.* A volume in **Natural Law Studies.**

78. Steven V. Hicks, *International Law and the Possibility of a Just World Order: An Essay on Hegel's Universalism.* A volume in **Universal Justice.**

79. E. F. Kaelin, *Texts on Texts and Textuality: A Phenomenology of Literary Art,* edited by Ellen J. Burns.

80. Amihud Gilead, *Saving Possibilities: A Study in Philosophical Psychology.* A volume in **Philosophy and Psychology.**

81. André Mineau, *The Making of the Holocaust: Ideology and Ethics in the Systems Perspective.* A volume in **Holocaust and Genocide Studies.**

82. Howard P. Kainz, *Politically Incorrect Dialogues: Topics Not Discussed in Polite Circles.*

83. Veikko Launis, Juhani Pietarinen, and Juha Räikkä, Editors, *Genes and Morality: New Essays.* A volume in **Nordic Value Studies.**

84. Steven Schroeder, *The Metaphysics of Cooperation: The Case of F. D. Maurice.*

85. Caroline Joan ("Kay") S. Picart, *Thomas Mann and Friedrich Nietzsche: Eroticism, Death, Music, and Laughter.* A volume in **Central-European Value Studies.**

86. G. John M. Abbarno, Editor, *The Ethics of Homelessness: Philosophical Perspectives.*

87. James Giles, Editor, *French Existentialism: Consciousness, Ethics, and Relations with Others.* A volume in **Nordic Value Studies.**

88. Deane Curtin and Robert Litke, Editors, *Institutional Violence.* A volume in **Philosophy of Peace.**

89. Yuval Lurie, *Cultural Beings: Reading the Philosophers of* Genesis.

90. Sandra A. Wawrytko, Editor, *The Problem of Evil: An Intercultural Exploration.* A volume in **Philosophy and Psychology.**

91. Gary J. Acquaviva, *Values, Violence, and Our Future.* A volume in **Hartman Institute Axiology Studies.**

92. Michael R. Rhodes, *Coercion: A Nonevaluative Approach.*

93. Jacques Kriel, *Matter, Mind, and Medicine: Transforming the Clinical Method.*

94. Haim Gordon, *Dwelling Poetically: Educational Challenges in Heidegger's Thinking on Poetry.* A volume in **Philosophy of Education.**

95. Ludwig Grünberg, *The Mystery of Values: Studies in Axiology,* edited by Cornelia Grünberg and Laura Grünberg.

96. Gerhold K. Becker, Editor, *The Moral Status of Persons: Perspectives on Bioethics.* A volume in **Studies in Applied Ethics.**

97. Roxanne Claire Farrar, *Sartrean Dialectics: A Method for Critical Discourse on Aesthetic Experience.*

98. Ugo Spirito, *Memoirs of the Twentieth Century.* Translated from Italian and edited by Anthony G. Costantini. A volume in **Values in Italian Philosophy.**

99. Steven Schroeder, *Between Freedom and Necessity: An Essay on the Place of Value.*

100. Foster N. Walker, *Enjoyment and the Activity of Mind: Dialogues on Whitehead and Education.* A volume in **Philosophy of Education.**

101. Avi Sagi, *Kierkegaard, Religion, and Existence: The Voyage of the Self.* Translated from Hebrew by Batya Stein.

102. Bennie R. Crockett, Jr., Editor, *Addresses of the Mississippi Philosophical Association.* A volume in **Histories and Addresses of Philosophical Societies.**

103. Paul van Dijk, *Anthropology in the Age of Technology: The Philosophical Contribution of Günther Anders.*

104. Giambattista Vico, *Universal Right.* Translated from Latin and edited by Giorgio Pinton and Margaret Diehl. A volume in **Values in Italian Philosophy.**

105. Judith Presler and Sally J. Scholz, Editors, *Peacemaking: Lessons from the Past, Visions for the Future.* A volume in **Philosophy of Peace.**

106. Dennis Bonnette, *Origin of the Human Species.* A volume in **Studies in the History of Western Philosophy.**

107. Phyllis Chiasson, *Peirce's Pragmatism: The Design for Thinking.* A volume in **Studies in Pragmatism and Values.**

108. Dan Stone, Editor, *Theoretical Interpretations of the Holocaust.* A volume in **Holocaust and Genocide Studies.**

109. Raymond Angelo Belliotti, *What Is the Meaning of Human Life?*

110. Lennart Nordenfelt, *Health, Science, and Ordinary Language,* with Contributions by George Khushf and K. W. M. Fulford.

111. Daryl Koehn, *Local Insights, Global Ethics for Business.* A volume in **Studies in Applied Ethics.**

112. Matti Häyry and Tuija Takala, Editors, *The Future of Value Inquiry.* A volume in **Nordic Value Studies.**

113. Conrad P. Pritscher, *Quantum Learning: Beyond Duality.*

114. Thomas M. Dicken and Rem B. Edwards, *Dialogues on Values and Centers of Value: Old Friends, New Thoughts.* A volume in **Hartman Institute Axiology Studies.**

115. Rem B. Edwards, *What Caused the Big Bang?* A volume in **Philosophy and Religion.**

116. Jon Mills, Editor, *A Pedagogy of Becoming.* A volume in **Philosophy of Education.**

117. Robert T. Radford, *Cicero: A Study in the Origins of Republican Philosophy.* A volume in **Studies in the History of Western Philosophy.**

118. Arleen L. F. Salles and María Julia Bertomeu, Editors, *Bioethics: Latin American Perspectives.* A volume in **Philosophy in Latin America.**

119. Nicola Abbagnano, *The Human Project: The Year 2000,* with an Interview by Guiseppe Grieco. Translated from Italian by Bruno Martini and Nino Langiulli. Edited with an Introduction by Nino Langiulli. A volume in **Studies in the History of Western Philosophy.**

120. Daniel M. Haybron, Editor, *Earth's Abominations: Philosophical Studies of Evil.* A volume in **Personalist Studies.**

121. Anna T. Challenger, *Philosophy and Art in Gurdjieff's* Beelzebub: *A Modern Sufi Odyssey.*

122. George David Miller, *Peace, Value, and Wisdom: The Educational Philosophy of Daisaku Ikeda.* A volume in **Daisaku Ikeda Studies.**

123. Haim Gordon and Rivca Gordon, *Sophistry and Twentieth-Century Art.*